IT'S ALL ABOUT LOVE

Don Menkens

Contents

Our love for our Saviour and Lord grows stronger as we get to know Him.

It is another example of God's LOVE, even implanted in His creatures!

FOREWORD

What is happening in our crazy world today? Where is **LOVE** being demonstrated?

There are so many wars in progress! Mega-rich men are striving to rule the world and **FORCING** people to follow their dictates or be severely punished or even put to death. Men are killing each other and committing so much evil and hate toward one another. So many people today are living in fear every day. Every passing day the news headlines report so much crime, even among our very young people. Rare diseases are increasing rapidly all over the world. In many countries, persecution of the true followers of the **Great I AM** is rampant!

Then there are so many disasters happening in the natural world with tornadoes, cyclones, fires, floods, earthquakes destroying homes and property leaving many homeless and many dead. These things are happening more and more frequently than ever before.

There are two empires at work in our world. There is the empire of the **Great I AM** which is ruled by **LOVE**, and the empire of **Lucifer**, which is ruled by **FORCE.** When will all this sin, suffering and death come to an end?

In this book, I try to show how this all came about, how and when it will end, and the vast difference between these two empires. May we all also see the abundant evidence of the Truth of God's Holy Word, and the **LOVING** offer of eternal life in a totally re-created earth where sin, suffering and death will never occur again.

FORCE is the very opposite of **LOVE**!

INTRODUCTORY STORY

"IT'S ALL ABOUT LOVE"!

Well, how can that be? Think about those you love. Your wife? Your children? Your parents? Your friends?

Would you do anything to hurt them? **NEVER!** Not if you love them. Would you force them to do anything against their will? **NEVER!**

You would warn them about possible consequences of their choices because you love them, but you would never force them to do what they really wanted to do, except perhaps when they are not old enough to know right from wrong.

Well, how do you determine right from wrong? Good question!

Why is it wrong to steal, to tell lies, to have sex with whosoever you choose, to kill others, to have no regard for your parents, or to lust after those things others have? Hmm! Where did these ideas come from?

My dear old Grandfather, at his hundredth birthday in Bowen, North Queensland, was asked what his advice for us would be? His answer was: **"Just follow the SEVEN WORD rule!**

"Oh", we said. "What's that Grandad?"

"DO AS YOU WOULD BE DONE BY."

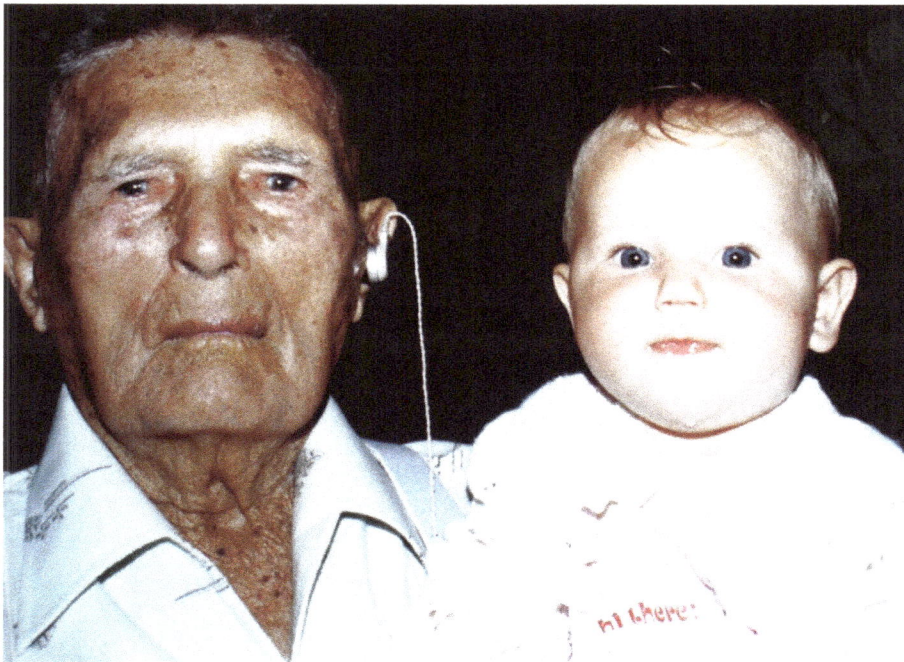

Grandad Menkens One Hundred Years Old, and my granddaughter Natalie, just one year old, at his birthday anniversary celebration in Bowen, North Queensland. He read his telegram from the Queen without his glasses!

"Do as you would be done by" sounds like what we call the "**Golden Rule**", or in other words, the rule of **LOVE**. It's all about **LOVE**! Where is that rule found? In a most amazing Book! So, let's explore this ancient Book and consider so many actual facts that show the truth of this Book, facts that show evidence of Truth in its pages. But first, let me share a remarkable love story:

A little boy's sister was dying of a rare disease and needed a blood transfusion urgently. The doctors could not find a donor who had the same blood type. They finally wondered if her little brother might have the same type and found that he did. So, his parents and the doctors explained the situation to him and the procedure to do the infusion and asked if he would be willing to give his blood to save his sister. He was very quiet for a while but then said he would do it.

The doctors did the infusion, and the sister seemed to improve almost immediately. The little chap again was very quiet for a few minutes and then asked,

"When will I die?"

What an amazing demonstration of love from a little five or six-year-old! He really believed that he was giving his life to save his sister!

Even the birds know It's about LOVE!

CHAPTER 1

HOW COULD THIS BE?

How could it be all about **LOVE** when we see so much evil and hate in our world?

I'd like to begin by comparing what an amazing ancient Book says with what Man says: **Creation** versus **Evolution**.

Question 1

Where did our world come from?

The Book says, "In the beginning an Almighty, Eternal, Omniscient Being created the heavens and the earth!" Genesis 1:1

Man says, "No! Not so! In the beginning there was a 'Big Bang', and over billions of years the universe has been gradually developing, to how it is today. Educated scientists at various universities, tell us, "It was an explosion of space itself. Starting from extremely high density and temperature, space expanded, the universe cooled, and the simplest elements formed. Gravity gradually drew matter together to form the first stars and the first galaxies. The "Big Bang" was the moment 13.8 billion years ago when the universe began as a tiny, dense, fireball that exploded. Most astronomers use the Big Bang theory to explain how the universe began. **But what caused this explosion in the first place is still a mystery**." See **"History of the Earth" article at Wikipedia. org** for more of man's ideas.

Interesting that Man says it is still a mystery.

Question 2

What was it like at first?

The Book says, "It was without form and void, and darkness was upon the face of the deep. And the Spirit of this Almighty Being moved upon the face of the waters. And He said, "Let there be light and there was light." Genesis 1: 2, 3.

Man says, "Gradually over billions of years the solar system formed with the planets, the sun and the moon. **The University at Buffalo in New York** speaks about Cosmic Inflation. Prior to the Big Bang, the universe underwent a breathtaking cosmic expansion doubling in size at least eighty times in a fraction of a second. This rapid inflation, fuelled by **a mysterious form of energy that permeated empty space, left the universe desolate and cold**."

Again, Man says it is "mysterious" how it all began!

Question 3

How did Day and Night come about?

The Book says, Genesis 1:4,5 "And this Almighty Eternal Being saw the light that it was good, and He divided the light from the darkness, and He called the light Day and the darkness He called Night. And the Evening and the Morning were the first Day!"

Man says, "Not sure how the names came about—**Day, Night, Evening, Morning,** but we admit that they were written in an ancient Book, and we do indeed still use them today."

Well, they have that correct, according to God's Word. That ancient book is His Word. It says the Creator provided the names Day, Night, Evening and Morning!

Question 4

How did the firmament come about?

The Book says, "And this Almighty Being said, "Let there be a firmament in the midst of the waters, and let it divide the waters from the waters. And He made the firmament and divided the waters which were under the firmament from the waters which were above the firmament: and it was so. And then He called the firmament Heaven. And the evening and the morning were the second day". Genesis 1:6,7,8

Man Says, the firmament just evolved over billions of years. All the stars, planets and galaxies just moved into their respective orbits, all rotating in perfect precision by chance over long periods of time. **"Wikipedia"** attributes the word Firmament to Bible Cosmology, in an article called "Firmament." It says the Firmament is the vast solid dome created by God during the **Genesis creation narrative,** to divide the primal sea into upper and lower portions so that the dry land could appear. The concept was adopted into the subsequent Classical/Medieval model of heavenly spheres but was dropped with advances in astronomy in the 16th and 17th centuries. Today it survives as a synonym for "sky" or "heaven".

Thank you! Now we know!

Question 5

How did the Earth, Seas and Oceans come about?

The Book says, "And the Almighty Being said, Let the waters under the Heaven be gathered together into one place, and let the dry land appear. And it was so. He called the dry land **Earth**, and the gathering together of the waters He called **Seas.** He saw that it was good."   Genesis 1:9,10

These words also, we still use today. The large Seas we call Oceans.

Man says, The **Earth, Seas and Oceans** gathered together over more billions of years to where they are today. We have no idea how the boundaries were actually fixed but "it has something to do with seafloor spreading and tectonic plates separating from one another", says **"National Geographic."**

Hmmm! Again, an interesting honest admission! God's Word says the Creator did it all!

Extra to Question 5. I remember on Guy Fawkes nights, or other special occasions, we sometimes used Firecrackers. We sent Skyrockets into the air, and yes, there was a "Big Bang" and fiery pieces flew all about. They then go out and fall to the Earth. I have never seen any pieces forming galaxies suspended in perfect precision like our planetary system which moves in precise paths perfectly timed to give us our years and seasons, months, and days. They all move in perfect timing.

Question 6

Where did the grass, herbs and trees with fruit and seeds come from?

The Book says, and this Almighty Being said, "Let the earth bring forth grass, the herb yielding seed, and the fruit tree yielding fruit after his kind, whose seed is in itself, upon the earth: and it was so.

And the earth brought forth grass, and herb yielding seed after his kind, and the tree yielding fruit, whose seed was in itself, after his kind: and He saw that it was good. And the evening and the morning were the third day."   Genesis 1: 11, 12,13.

Man says, No one knows how this actually happened, but it came about after billions of years of slowly evolving. **"ChatGPT"** says, "Oxygen came first. Trees, and other plants produce oxygen through the process of photosynthesis. This process has been taking place on earth for billions of years, long before the first trees or other land plants appeared."

Hmmm! Again, where is the <u>credible</u> evidence to support such an assumption!

Question 7

How did our planetary system come about with the sun, moon and planets, all moving in perfect precision, for our years, for signs and seasons?

The Book says, Again, this Almighty Being said, "Let there be lights in the firmament of the heaven to divide the day from the night; and let them be for signs, and for seasons, and for days and years: and let them be for lights in the firmament of the heaven, to give light upon the earth: He made two great lights; the greater light to rule the day, and the lesser light to rule the night; he made the stars also. He saw that it was good, and the evening and the morning were the fourth day." Genesis 1:19.

Man says, all these lights in the heavens, the sun, moon and stars, all came from the "Big Bang" that happened billions of years ago. **"Space.com"** says, "In a wide expanse of space, gravity drew dust and gas together to create the young solar system. The sun formed first from the vast material, with the planets close behind. Most of the material in space is filled with dust and gas. It contains mostly hydrogen and helium. About **4.5 billion years ago**, waves of energy travelling through space, pressed clouds of such particles together, and gravity caused them to collapse in on themselves and then start to spin. These are the first steps of how the solar system formed."

Hmmm! Such an improbable hypothesis, again with no credible evidence to support such an assertion.

Question 8

How did all the different fish, fowls, beasts and cattle develop?

The Book says, This Omniscient Being said, "Let the waters bring forth abundantly, the moving creature that has life, and fowl that may fly above the earth in the open firmament of heaven. He created great **whales**, and every living creature that moves, which the waters brought forth abundantly, after their kind, and every winged **fowl** after his kind: and He blessed them, saying, Be fruitful and multiply and fill the waters in the seas, and let the fowl multiply in the earth, and He saw that it was good. And the evening and the morning were the fifth day." Genesis 1: 20-23.

Man says, all this happened over billions of years. The animals, fish and birds gradually changed, or evolved, into higher forms as we see them today. **"Understanding Evolution"**, says, "It happened through macroevolution through ecograms! Tetrapods means four feet and includes all creatures today that have four feet, but it also includes many animals that don't have four feet. All birds and humans are tetrapods, because they descend from the tetrapod ancestor, even if they have secondarily lost their four feet."

Hmmm! I've never seen a cat change into a dog or vice versa; or a hen evolve into an emu. I've never seen a four-footed animal change into a bird or a fish. Have you? Where's the evidence?

Recently I found a very interesting article**, in a book titled "Jonah and the Whale"**, by Charles G. Bellah which again shows the Truth of God's Word and His mighty Power.

Jonah's story is found in the Book of Jonah in the Old Testament. God told him to go to the city of Ninevah and warn them to stop their evil behaviour. Jonah did not want to do that as it was a very wicked city! So, he boarded a ship to go to Joppa, far away from Ninevah.

During the journey a huge storm arose, and Jonah realized that they would all be shipwrecked and drown. Realizing that God had arranged the storm to wake him up, he told the sailors to throw him overboard. They did this and the storm stopped, but what happened to Jonah?

The story says a huge whale swallowed Jonah, who ended up in the whale's belly. Sometime later, (the story says three days and three nights in its belly), the whale vomited Jonah out on to the sand near Ninevah. He was still alive and after recovering somewhat, he decided to obey God and went to Ninevah to deliver God's warning.

Now many people say this is impossible, but this article shows that it is surely possible to have a "holiday" in a whale's belly and survive! Here's the article from **"Jonah and the Whale"** in which the author quotes a story from **"Literary Digest"** published 4th April,1896. It shows it is indeed possible for a man to be swallowed by a whale and still survive!

One day in February,1891, the whaling ship "State of the East", launched two small boats with men and harpoons to go after a huge whale not far off. The men were successful in harpooning the whale and capturing it, but as it struggled, one of the boats was struck by the tail of the whale and smashed to pieces. The men were thrown into the ocean.

Eventually, all but two of the men were saved by the men in the other boat, and later, the body of one of the other two men was found. But the other, James Bartley, could not be found anywhere!

It took a day and a half to get the huge whale onto the deck and cut up. Then they cut open the big stomach, and there was James Bartley, unconscious, but still alive! For several days he was delirious, and it was three weeks before he recovered his reason and could tell about his terrible experience. But he lived for many years afterwards.

Other stories and experiences of men and huge fish, and even of a horse being found in a whale's stomach are given in the book, **"Jonah and the Whale"**!

Question 9

Now the big question! How did man and woman come to be?

The Book says, this amazing Almighty, Eternally Existing, Omnipotent, Omniscient, Omnipresent Being, said, "Let us make **man** in our image, after our likeness: and let them have dominion over the fish of the sea, and over the fowl of the air, and over the cattle, and over all the earth, and over every creeping thing that creeps upon the earth." When **Adam** came forth from the Creator's hand, he bore, in his physical, mental, and spiritual nature, a likeness to his Maker. God created man in His own image, and it was His purpose that the longer man lived the more fully he would reveal this image—the more fully reflect the glory of the Creator. So, He created man in His own image, in the image of Himself He created him; **male** and **female** He created them. And He blessed them, and said, "Be fruitful, and multiply, and replenish the earth, and subdue it: and have dominion over the fish of the sea, and over the fowl of the air, and over every living thing that moves upon the earth." Genesis 1:26,27,28.

Man says, "Man and woman slowly developed over billions of years, maybe from some slime that slithered out of a swamp, and gradually developed in different ways, into higher forms such as insects, and small creatures, and gradually they developed into higher and higher forms, again, over long periods of time. Those higher forms gradually developed into animals and birds and fish. Some of those creatures which looked like a man, the monkeys and apes, gradually developed into a man and woman. One source, the **"University of Pittsburgh"**, says, "These early stages are not completely understood, because the majority of animal species developed into the arguably less titillating separate sex state too long ago, for scientists to observe the transition."

Hmmm! Here's an interesting anecdote example of the evolutionary theory.

Two students at a university were thinking of this!

One asked the other if his mother was an ape? The other student became angry.

"I take that as a NO! Then was your grandmother an ape?"

Another angry "NO!"!

"What about your great grandmother?" and so on...

No answer, and a stormy exit!

As one commentator put it, Man says, **"It was _Goo_ to _Zoo_ to _You!_"**

I really don't think so!

Question 10

How long did it take for this Almighty, Eternal Being to complete all His work of Creation?

The Book says, "And He saw everything that He had made, and behold, it was all very good. And the evening and the morning were the sixth day." Genesis 2:31.

Man says, No! No! It took millions and millions of years to get to where we are today. It all just evolved gradually over billions of years! **"Space.com"** says, **4.5 billion years ago.** See their whole statement at Question 7.

Again, where is the evidence for this statement?

Question 11

How did all the animals, birds and fish get their names?

The Book says, "And out of the ground, this Almighty Being made every beast of the field and every fowl of the air and brought them to Adam to see what he would call them; and whatever Adam called every living creature, that was the name thereof." Genesis 2:19,20.

Man says, we have no idea how all the creatures on earth, the air and the sea, got their names. Maybe a professor or scientist gave them the names they have today.

Hmmm! They have this answer as a possibility, that it may have been some scientist or professor. Where are these scientists or professors recorded? A Lion has always been a Lion. A Whale has always been a Whale, and an Eagle likewise!

Question 12

What was provided as food for the animals, birds and fish?

The Book says, "And to every beast of the field, and to every fowl of the air, and to everything that creeps upon the earth, wherein there is life, I have given every green herb for meat: and it was so." Genesis 1:30 and Isaiah 65:25.

Man says, the animals, birds and fish started eating whatever they fancied, developing their own digestive systems as billions of years passed. **"Active Wild"** says, "There are three kinds of digestive systems; carnivores, (lions eat other animals), omnivores, (bears eat animals like fish, as well as fruit, nuts and honey), and herbivores, (cattle eat only grass). There are also fructivores, (fruit eaters), and folivores, (leaf eaters).

There is no evidence that I can find from man, as to how the various diets came about.

Question 13

What was provided for man to eat as food?

The Book says, This Almighty, Omniscient Being said to Adam, "Behold I have given you every herb bearing seed which is upon the face of all the earth, and every tree, in which is the fruit of a tree yielding seed, to you it shall be for meat." Genesis 1:29

Man says, man developed a digestive system that could eat whatever they fancied. Some **chose** to eat fruit, vegetables, and seeds, while some **chose** to eat the flesh of other creatures as well.

"Andrews and Martin 1991", say, "The diet of early hominins was probably somewhat similar to the diet of chimpanzees: omnivorous, including large quantities of fruit, leaves, flowers, bark, insects and meat."

I'm glad my father and mother were not eaten!

Question 14

When did man begin to eat vegetables growing in the field?

The Book says, this Great, Almighty Being said sadly, because you have chosen to listen to My enemy, and disobey My specific instructions not to eat of a certain tree, thorns and thistles shall the earth bring forth, and you shall eat the <u>herb of the field.</u> Genesis 3:18-19.

Man says, man just chose to eat whatever he liked. Some chose to eat vegetables, and some chose other foods like flesh, or whatever they fancied. In **"Human Origins",** (Smithsonian Institution), it says, "The major evolutionary change in the human diet, was the incorporation of meat and marrow from large animals which occurred by at least 2.6 million years ago."

Hmmm!

Where is some credible evidence, please?

Question 15

How did a woman come about?

The Book says, and the Almighty Being said, "It is not good for man to be alone. I will make a helpmeet for him. And He caused a deep sleep to fall upon Adam, and he slept; and He took one of his ribs and closed up the flesh thereof. And the rib which He had taken from man, He made woman. And brought her unto the man. And Adam said, this is now bone of my bones, and flesh of my flesh: she shall be called Woman, because she was taken out of man. And they were both naked and were not ashamed." Genesis 2:18 to 25.

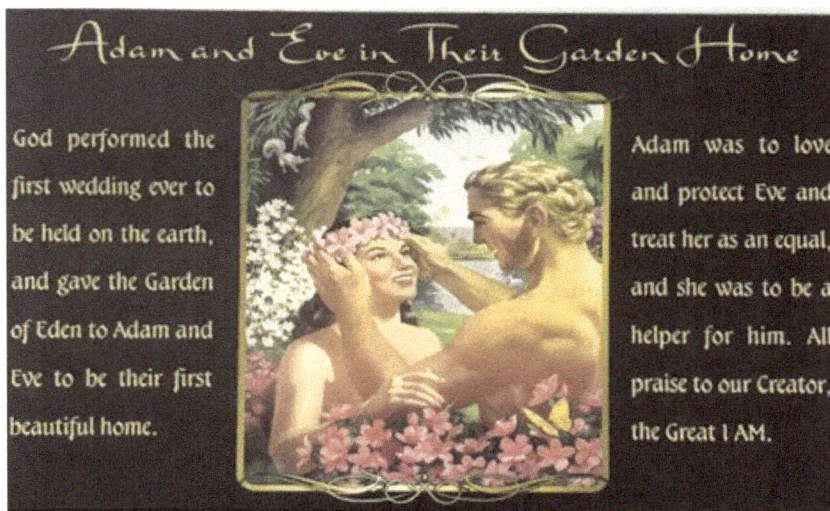

Adam and Eve in Their Garden Home

God performed the first wedding ever to be held on the earth, and gave the Garden of Eden to Adam and Eve to be their first beautiful home.

Adam was to love and protect Eve and treat her as an equal, and she was to be a helper for him. All praise to our Creator, the Great I AM.

Man says, over billions of years man became tired and lonely, and so he developed a beautiful woman for himself, just like all other life forms. **"Seattle Times"** says, "According to scientists, the very first organisms to engage in sex were more like Adam and Steve than Adam and Eve. The first sexual beings to emerge perhaps 2.5 million years ago, were what scientists call isogamous— which is a little like being gay, except everyone is between male and female." Hmmm!

Evidence needed please!

Recently, I came across another interesting anecdote, where some monkeys were discussing the origin of man, which I found amusing:

Three monkeys sat on a coconut tree,

Discussing things as they're said to be.

Said one to the other,

"Now listen you two,

There's a certain rumour

That can't be true …

That man descended from our noble race.

The very idea is sure to disgrace."

"No monkey ever deserted his wife,

Starved her babies and ruined her life.

And you've never known another monk,

To leave her babies with others to bunk,

Or pass them on from one to another."

"And another thing you will never see …

Is a monk build a fence around a coconut tree,

And let the coconuts go to waste,

Forbidding all the other monks to taste."

"Why, if I put a fence around this tree,

Starvation would force you to steal from me."

"And here's something else a monk won't do .Go out
at night and get on a stew;

Or use a gun or club or knife,

To take some other monkey's life."

"Yes, man descended … ornery cuss,

But, brother, … he didn't descend from us!

Question 16

How long did it take for the Great Omnipotent Being to do all His creating?

The Books says, "And He saw everything that He had made, and behold it was very good. And the evening and the morning were the sixth day." Genesis 1:31

Man says, it all took billions of years for everything to develop to what we see today. Man is becoming more and more intelligent and now has made all sorts of inventions like motor vehicles, aeroplanes that can carry hundreds of passengers, huge ships like floating cities, wonderful communication equipment and on and on. **"Sage"** says, "The Earth is estimated to have formed around 4.5 million years ago. This is based on **scientific evidence,** including the study of rock formations, and the age of the moon."

Hmmm! Where is this credible "scientific evidence"?

For about six thousand years, men have travelled by foot or using animals. Weapons were swords, bows and arrows and spears. Just in my short lifetime of nearly ninety years, we see the Truth of God's Word as in Daniel chapter 12 that "Knowledge shall be increased, and men shall run to and fro".

This did not happen over long periods of time!

We'll look at some of the amazing modern means of travel, and increase of knowledge **just in my lifetime,** in a forthcoming chapter.

Question 17

What did the Eternal, Almighty Creator do after He finished all His work on the sixth day?

The Book says, "Thus the heavens and the earth were finished, and all the host of them. And on the seventh day, He rested from all His work that He had made; And He blessed the seventh day and sanctified it because that in it He had rested from all His work which He had created and made." Genesis 2:1,2,3.

Man says, that's all-fairy tales. It took billions of years to get to where we are today! And it is not finished yet. Man will continue to develop more and more intelligent, inventive and resourceful, and who knows how it will all end up?

"Your Genome" says, "Modern humans originated in Africa within the past 200,000 years and evolved from their **most likely** recent common ancestor, Homo erectus."

Hmmm! Most likely? No credible evidence given.

God's Word has the answer to that question! Check out I Thessalonians 4:13-18, and 1 Corinthians 15:52-55, as well as the rest of the Bible.

Question 18

What did this Wonderful, Creative Being say about the seventh day, Saturday we call it now, when He rested from all His work?

The Book says, "Remember the Sabbath day, the seventh day of the week, which I have sanctified, and keep it holy. Six days you shall do all your work, but the seventh day is the Sabbath of the Lord thy God. In it thou shalt not do any work, you, your son or daughter, your man servant, or your maidservant, nor thy stranger that is within thy gates. For in six days the Lord made heaven and earth, the sea and all that in them is, and rested the seventh day, wherefore the Lord blessed the seventh day and hallowed it." Exodus 20: 8 to 11.

Man says, you don't need to make the seventh day as a special Sabbath day. We have arranged for everyone to keep Sunday as a special day. Forget what this God says and do as you please every day, especially on Sunday, the first day of the week. We are the lords of the earth. We are in control of the earth, developing it to be even better and better. So, we should honour ourselves and do whatever pleases us, for we have developed into superior beings as you see us today.

The Roman emperor Constantine1, (died 337 AD), a convert to Christianity, introduced the first civil legislation concerning Sunday in 321 AD. Check any library for this history.

Hmmm!

Again, it's a matter of <u>choice</u>. I wasn't present when God created the heavens and the earth! However, the Genesis account is definitely the more credible to me! Because I love and trust my Heavenly Father, I will keep His commands and remember Him as my <u>Creator</u> on His special day—<u>the seventh day of the week; His Sabbath Day.</u>

For more information on Evolution, check out **Charles Darwin** and his book **"Origin of Species"**. He is known as the "Father of the Evolution theory". His studies and "evidence" are in direct contrast to the Word of God in the Bible. I have often wondered why Darwin could possibly devise such a thesis as Evolution.

Apparently, Charles and his wife had a lovely daughter who was a bright, beautiful and gracious child who loved her parents dearly. When she was about ten years old, she contracted a serious illness which ended her life. Her parents were heart-broken and went to the priest for some consolation in their grief.

In April 1851, Annie, the beloved daughter of Charles and Emma Darwin died at 10 years of age after an extended illness.

Charles decided not to attend her funeral because he believed he would gain no comfort from a Christian service, especially as she was not baptised and he was told she would suffer eternal torment.

The priest asked them if she had been baptized. The parents told him they had not had that done yet. **The priest then told them that their daughter would burn in hell for eternity!**

Can you imagine how they were aghast at his pronouncement. No wonder they wanted nothing to do with such a hateful cruel being, and looked for some other explanation of how the world came to be, instead of a loving Creator God! **Heiligman p.231**

Why did God tell us in the fourth commandment, to **"Remember the Sabbath Day to keep it holy? Six days thou shalt work, but the seventh day is the Sabbath of the Lord thy God."** On that day, **which is what we call Saturday now**, His people are to rest and **REMEMBER** that He is their **CREATOR and REDEEMBER.**

Man says we will dispense with this commandment and keep Sunday because Jesus rose from the tomb on Sunday. **There is no Scripture supporting this idea which arose from an edict by a pagan Roman emperor!**

Why do the majority of "Christians" keep the nine commandments, but dispense with the fourth commandment which identifies Who our Heavenly Father is?

Note: Today, it is difficult to purchase a diary or calendar which starts with Sunday, as the first Day of the week as it has been for nearly six thousand years. Calendars and Diaries now start on Monday, thus making Sunday the seventh day. **It's just another lie of Lucifer, with most of the Christian churches unknowingly worshipping God on Satan's false sabbath!**

When asked which is the greatest commandment, Jesus said, **"Love the Lord your God with all your heart, and with all your soul and with all your mind. This is the first and greatest commandment. And the second is like it: Love your neighbour as yourself."** Matthew 22: 36-40

Jesus also says very plainly, **"If you love Me, keep My commandments… He who has My commandments and keeps them, it is he who loves Me…If anyone loves Me, he will keep My Word; and My Father will love him, and We will come to him and make Our home with him."** John 14: 15-24

My wife and I keep the seventh day Sabbath, (now called Saturday), because we love God supremely, and want to please Him with all our heart, and mind and strength. He is our loving Heavenly Father who loves all His vast Creation.

What a Master Artist is our loving Creator God!

CHAPTER 2

FREE WILL TO CHOOSE

Well, by now you surely have realized that this amazing Book, is God's sacred Word, the Scriptures, or as we know it—the Bible, and the Almighty, Eternally Existing, Omnipotent, Omniscient, Omnipresent Being, is the **LORD GOD**!

"Let all the earth fear the Lord: Let all the inhabitants of the earth stand in awe of Him. For He just speaks, and it is done. He commands and it stands fast." Psalms 33:8,9.

What an amazing, wonderful Being is the Lord, my Creator and Redeemer.

He gives to every one of his created beings, his own **freewill to choose** whether to obey His commands, and accept the salvation He offers freely, giving us **"an endless hope"**, instead of a **"hopeless end!"**

I don't know how He began or how He existed before He made the world and everything in it. I am just one of His created beings, but I surely love Him for who He is. I **choose** to honour Him instead of **choosing** to believe that everything just happened by chance over billions of years!

He does nothing for us without our cooperation. He loves His creation, but He is not a God of **force**. He gives every man and woman the right to make their own **choices**. He is a God of **love**.

It's all about love!

When Adam and Eve **chose** to believe the Serpent in the Garden of Eden, they **chose** to reject God and follow the Serpent's lies, thus breaking God's specific instructions, His law, that He made plain to them in the Garden of Eden.

Even then He had a plan in place for man to **choose** to be saved for His Kingdom. His Son, Jesus, the Word, had agreed with His Father, to follow a plan which would offer salvation to all men and women.

It is a wonderful demonstration of who the Lord is. He is not a God of **force** like the leaders of this world who are planning to set up a New World Order, a United Nations, a World Health Organization, where everyone will have to **choose** whether to obey man-made laws, or face punishment.

He says in His Word, Matthew 11: 28-30:

"Come unto Me, all ye that labour and are heavy laden, and I will give you rest. Take My yoke upon you and learn of Me; for I am meek and lowly of heart: and ye shall find rest unto your souls."

It was Jesus Who said these much loved and much quoted words:

"For God so loved the world, that He gave His only begotten Son, that whosoever believeth in Him should not perish but have everlasting life. For God sent not His Son into the world to condemn the world; but that the world through Him might be saved." (John 3: 16,17.)

What an incredibly wonderful loving God He is. Even these birds agree!

What a beautiful example of LOVE!

CHAPTER 3

AN ARCHEOLOGIST'S FINDINGS

God's Word is so precious to me. Over and over, it can be shown that it is true, and I'd like to relate some ways in which it can be proven to be Truth!

Unlike the Evolutionary Theory, evidence of the Truth of God's Word, the BIBLE, is overwhelming! If His Word can be proven true, should I not believe that He is truly our **Creator** and **Redeemer?**

1. The great Flood of Noah's day.

An anaesthetist from the United States, wanted to check out the truth of what the Bible says about this huge flood which the Word says destroyed all life on our planet because God saw how wicked His created beings had become.

His name was Ron Wyatt. He would work at different hospitals for half the year to fund his plans, and then he travelled to the far east and spent the rest of the year, often with his sons, to see if he could find evidence of the Bible story.

He indeed found the almost rotted away remains of a great ship, on the sides of Mount Ararat in Turkey. It matched the measurements that are given in God's Word. See Genesis 6: 14-17. The remains matched the measurements God gave Noah in cubits, as given in God's Word! God said to make it of Gopher Wood. It had to have rooms in it, and was to be 300 cubits long, (that's 137.16m in our measurements today.) It was to be 50 cubits wide, (that's 24.1m) and 30 cubits high. (13.72m.) It was to have many rooms and three decks high. It was to be pitched within and without with pitch.

Wow! Now that's a huge ship!

The Turkish Government have built a Museum and a Tourist Centre nearby for tourists to come and see for themselves the remains of this great ship!

2. The real Mount Sinai or Horeb as it was also called.

There are many references to Mount Sinai in the Bible, but one in the New Testament is found in Galatians 4:25, where Paul speaks of **Mount Sinai <u>in Arabia.</u>** In most Bibles Mount Sinai is shown in the Sinai Peninsula. The Roman Emperor Constantine sent his mother Helena, to find the location of Mount Sinai, and she says it is not in Arabia but in the Sinai Peninsula. The Bible says it is in <u>Saudi Arabia!</u>

Also in Arabia is a mountain called **Jabal al Lawz** with a very blackened summit, where Moses was given **the Law, the Ten Commandments <u>from God, written by God in stone by His own fiery finger, twice</u>! It is the only part of the Bible that God actually wrote! <u>How important then, is God's Holy Law of Ten Commandments!</u>**

3. *The Red Sea Crossing.*

The Bible says God led the Israelites out of Egypt and brought them through a valley with mountains on either side, to a huge beach on the western side of the Gulf of Aqaba.

The Egyptians changed their intentions about letting the Israelites go, for they had them as slaves for many years. They gathered an army with horses and chariots to follow the Israelites and bring them back to Egypt. The Israelite people realized the Egyptians were following them and became very afraid and cried out to Moses.

God told Moses to smite waters with his staff, and God miraculously opened the sea allowing the people to cross safely to the other side, on dry ground.

The Egyptians followed and when they were all part way across with their chariots and horses, God told Moses to smite the waters again with his staff and the waters closed up, and all the Egyptians with their horses and chariots were drowned. This is the Bible story which can be found in Exodus 14.

What an incredible story of salvation for the Israelite people! Again, an example of God's love and concern for His people.

It's all about love!

Ron and his sons found this huge beach, called Nuweiba, and decided to dive to see if they could find any evidence of what happened there according to the Bible account.

They found an underwater ridge not far below the surface, with steep depths on either side of it. The water was quite clear, and they noticed strange formations embedded in the coral. On closer examination they found that they were the remains of chariot wheels, some with six spokes and some with four. Also, they found the remains of horses and men also embedded in the coral all along the sea bed. Ron was able to take photographs of what they found.

Thus, the Bible has proved true once again, irrefutable evidence that you can go and see for yourself if you have a mind to. You can read the whole account in Exodus 14:21-31.

4. *Sodom and Gomorrah.*

The reason why these cities and three others nearby were destroyed, is given in Genesis 13:12 and 13. The people had become exceedingly wicked with no regard for any laws, love for God or their neighbours.

(It is very similar today with murders and thefts and all sorts of wicked things on the news nearly every night.)

In Genesis 19: 24, and 25, the Bible account says, "The Lord rained upon Sodom and Gomorrah brimstone and fire from the Lord out of heaven. He overthrew those cities, and all the plain, and all the inhabitants of the cities, and that which grew upon the ground."

Ron visited the site of those ancient cities and again photographed them. It still has the remains of streets and buildings which can be clearly seen.

Some years ago, my wife and I were visiting with some dear friends who have also visited these sites, and they showed us some of the thousands of sulphur balls buried in the ashes.

Again, plain, clear evidence of the truth of the Bible, an amazing Book! Another proof of the truth of God's Word. It also shows that there is a limit to God's patience and love.

To protect those who love Him and keep His commandments, He sometimes has to do things that He would rather not do, to protect those of His children who truly love Him for who He is-- a God of love!

It's all about LOVE… God's LOVE for His people!

CHAPTER 4

BACKGROUND TO UNDERSTAND

Now the most amazing proof of the truth of God's Word!

Quite a few years ago, a good friend, Alan Edwards, who lived in Kingaroy, Queensland, gave me one of those old-time small tapes titled "Chariot Wheels", to listen to. On it was the story of a chap called Henry Groover, who believed it was his calling by God to travel the world telling anyone who would listen about the Gospel.

He tells how he met Ron Wyatt while he was visiting Jerusalem. They both were staying in the same hotel and Ron told Henry about his findings of Noah's Ark, the real Mount Sinai, the Red Sea Crossing, and the remains of Sodom and Gomorrah.

He also told Henry how he had found the Ark of the Covenant, in which Moses had placed the two stone tablets of the Ten Commandments, **written by God's own fiery finger, twice! Again, this is the only part of the Bible which was written by God Himself. <u>How important His Law, the Ten Commandments, must be!</u>**

God had told Moses to have a temple built with two rooms. The first room was called the Holy Place. In it were the Menorah, (the seven branched candlestick), the Altar of Incense, and the Table of Shewbread. Then, there was the Most Holy Place, where the Ark of the Covenant was to be placed The Ark was made of shittim wood and was overlaid with pure gold. It had a top with two angels covering it with their wings.

The High Priest would enter this Most Holy Place, before the Lord, once a year on the Day of Atonement, before the Ark of the Covenant, to sprinkle the blood of a sacrificed lamb, over the Ark of the Covenant, which contained the two tablets of stone on which was written the **Ten Commandments**.

The original promise to Adam and Eve, after they had disobeyed God and chose to believe and follow Satan's lies in the Garden of Eden, would be fulfilled. See Genesis 3 and especially verse 15.

Speaking about Satan, God said, "I will put enmity between thee and the woman, and between thy seed, (wicked people), and her seed; it (the seed of the woman, Jesus,) shall bruise thy head, and thou (Satan), shall bruise His heel.

The Temple and the sacrificial system were put in place by God, to show that the Lamb of God, Jesus Christ, would be sacrificed to pay the price, of sin! In the Courtyard, was the Altar of Burnt Offerings and the Laver of water.

The first apartment of the sanctuary was the Holy Place where the Menorah was placed, (the Seven Golden Candlesticks), showing Jesus as the Light of the world, the Altar of Incense, representing the Good News of Salvation and rising prayers to God. Lastly was the Table of Shew Bread, (Jesus, the Bread of Life).

In the second apartment was the Ark of the Covenant containing the Tables of Stone with Ten Commandments inscribed on them. There were two angels with wings outstretched over the Ark.

One day Jesus would come to the earth, and be sacrificed on a cross on Calvary, as the Lamb of God, to provide **PAYMENT IN FULL**, for the sins of the whole world: for whoever would **choose** to accept His free gift of **love**!

The sacrifice of an innocent lamb on the Day of Atonement once each year, with the High Priest taking the blood of the lamb, and sprinkling it over the Ark, demonstrated what Jesus, the innocent Lamb of God would do to atone for our sin.

Anyone who **chooses** to love and serve God, could look forward to an "endless hope", of eternal life in an earth made new with no more sin, suffering, pain or death, instead of a "hopeless end"!

Jesus would be sacrificed as the Lamb of God, Who takes away the sin of the world. Jesus Christ, the sinless Lamb of God, the Father's only begotten Son, would take our punishment, to set us free.

During the early days of settlement in America, Negro people from Africa were captured, chained, and brought to America, to be auctioned as slaves to men who needed labourers for their plantations.

At one auction there was a very strong, outstanding Negro, who was loudly making known that he would not work for any man! He was chief among his tribesmen in Africa, and he kept assuring the buyers that he would not work for any man.

The prices being offered became higher and higher till finally the auctioneer's hammer fell, and he was sold to the highest bidder for a very high price!

As the buyer led the chained Negro away, he kept on telling his buyer that he would not work for him, for he was a very important chief.

When they were far enough away from the crowd, the buyer stooped down and undid his chains and said, **"I didn't buy you to be my slave. I bought you at such a high price, to set you free!"**

The Negro was quiet for a while, but when he realized what this man had done for him, his response was, **"Oh Master! Thank you! Thank you! Thank you! I will love and serve you all the days of my life."**

Isn't this how our response should be, when we realize what a high price Jesus and the Father paid to set us free? What incredible love from our awesome God!

It's all about LOVE!

CHAPTER 5

PAID IN FULL!

Now let's go back to Ron Wyatt and Henry Groover, in Jerusalem. Ron continued telling Henry about finding the Ark of the Covenant. He told him how, at the time Babylon was approaching to capture Jerusalem, the prophet Jeremiah and some other faithful Jewish people helping, had taken the Ark of the Covenant with some other items from the temple and secreted it all in a cave under the very place where Jesus was to be crucified, and they did this at least seven hundred years before the events on Calvary!

Ron told how he had found the cave with a crack in the rock in the ceiling of the cave, right under the cross hole where Jesus was crucified which still had blood staining the rock.

After Jesus died, a Roman soldier pushed a spear into Jesus's side, and blood and water came forth. The record of all this is found in the Gospels. A great earthquake had split the rock at the foot of the cross, right above the Ark in the cave below. Jesus's blood flowed down that crack right onto the Tables of Stone of God's Holy Law. This was like the High Priest did in the Most Holy Place each year on the day of Atonement! The Jewish sacrificial system was fulfilled, and no longer needed. The price for our salvation was **paid in full!**

How incredible a story! When I first heard this on the tape, the hair on the back of my neck literally stood up, and I was so shocked that someone could make up such a story. I could not believe it was true and put it in the "impossible basket!"

Sometime later, we heard that Ron Wyatt was coming out to Australia to run some seminars about his findings. My wife and I drove to Toowoomba to hear what he had to say, and we couldn't fault his presentation. He seemed like a very truthful person, so we also travelled to Brisbane where he again had a presentation. I spoke with him personally and shook his hand. Again, I could not fault his honesty, and integrity. I was still not ready however, to accept the story about the Ark being placed by Jeremiah in a cave right under the cross-hole where Jesus was crucified, and Jesus's blood flowing down that crack in the rock right onto the Law of God given to Moses. I couldn't help thinking about it and wondering if it could possibly be true.

Sometime later, while we were minding a home in Camden, for some friends who were visiting relatives in Tasmania, I called another friend who lived near the coast, and related the story that Ron told us of his claim to have found the Ark of the Covenant in a cave under the cross-hole.

He said that what I had related was very interesting. He told me how his wife was from Arnhem Land in the Northern Territory. He told me how they sometimes travelled up there to visit her relatives in a little village called Maningrida. In this village, was a small church. On the back wall of the church, an aboriginal man, Nicholas Pascoe, had painted a picture of what was very like what Ron was claiming, with the Morning Stars announcing the birth of Jesus. Next was a scene of Jesus in the Bethlehem Manger, and then the Crucifixion Scene.

Under the centre cross where Jesus's body hung on the cross, Nicholas had painted a cave with a box in it, and Jesus's blood flowing down onto it.

Again, I was in total shock! How could an aboriginal man who had never seen Ron or read his books, paint such a graphic picture of what Ron had shared with his audiences, and what I had heard on that small tape? I asked my friend if he could send me a picture of the painting. In due course, he sent me the picture as shown below.

Nicholas Pascoe MANINGRIDA NT 0822
Morning Star announcing birth of Jesus
Jesus in Bethelem Manger
Illustration demonstrating Nicky's dreaming connecting
him to Jesus
Jesus on the cross at Calvary

What an awesome loving God, Who has His plans in place, even to the minutest details!

CHAPTER 6

ABOUT THE BLOOD OF JESUS

Ron was able to take some of the blood to a laboratory in Jerusalem to have it analysed. **It showed twenty-three "X" chromosomes which come from a mother but only one "Y" chromosome, from the father of the baby.**

When Mary, who was betrothed to Joseph, realised she was pregnant, the Lord spoke to Joseph and told him not to be troubled that Mary was pregnant before they were married, because her baby was conceived by the Holy Spirit.

To my humble understanding, if the father provides a "Y" chromosome the baby will be a boy. If the father provides another "X" chromosome the baby will be a girl. The blood from the cave ceiling showed twenty-three "X" chromosomes and only one "Y" chromosome. So, the baby Jesus, had His mother's "twenty-three "X" chromosomes" but only one "Y" chromosome", which meant He would be a boy. A normal human baby has forty-six chromosomes, so Jesus was a very special baby boy.

Jesus was the only begotten of the Father. He had a Human Nature and a Divine Nature! He was the innocent **"Lamb slain from the foundation of the world."** Revelation 13:8 and John 1:29.

And that is not all that was found. The blood sample was **still live blood**! Wow! How could that be? How could His blood not see corruption after 2000 years?

That fits with the Scriptures, in Psalm 16:10 which states clearly, **"Thou wilt not leave My soul in hell, neither wilt thou suffer Thine Holy One to see corruption."** Also check Leviticus 17:11-14, and Acts 13:35, which say, **"the life of the flesh is in the blood."** This is so incredible but true!

This is also why Jesus, at the Last Supper, said to His disciples, "This bread is my body which is broken for you. The wine is my blood which I shed for you." Check with these Scriptures. Matthew 26:17-29, Mark 12:25, Luke 22:7-38 and 1 Corinthians 11:23-25.

How incredible is our Omnipotent, Omniscient and Omnipresent God! He did all this because He loves His created beings, even the hardest and cruellest person. He loves everyone and offers salvation to anyone who will by faith, **choose** to accept and believe in Him.

What amazing love! Our God is not a God of force!

I LOVE you!

CHAPTER 7

LOVE DEMONSTRATED!

I'd like now to share another Old Testament story that also is truly amazing!

In the Book of Genesis chapter 18 the Lord promises that Abraham, who was a righteous man and who loved the Lord, that He would give him a wonderful land and a huge family. Abraham was one hundred years old and Sarah his wife was ninety odd. Though they were both very old without any children, God said they would have a son. You can read it all there in chapter 18, verses 9-15, and how Sarah laughed about it!

Well, in due course, as God had promised, Sarah became pregnant and had a baby boy. They named him Isaac, and they were so happy to have a son even in their old age! You can read about it in Genesis 21: 1-8.

The heathen nations round where Abraham and Sarah lived, were throwing some of their children into fires and doing other abominable things with their children, to supposedly please their pagan gods of wood and stone.

God wanted to show Abraham how one day, He would send his only Son, Jesus, to earth, to be sacrificed to atone for our sins, and the sins of the world. So, He told Abraham to take Isaac, his only son, and offer him as a sacrifice to Him, on Mount Moriah, where Jesus was sacrificed many years later.

Can you imagine how Abraham must have felt to take the only son he had in his old age, and kill him as a sacrifice to God? How could he have a huge family if he killed his only son, and what a shocking, terrible thing to ask Abraham to do! Again, you can read about it all in Genesis 22: 1-14.

Some read this story and reject God immediately, as it seems such a horrible thing to ask Abraham to do.

But Abraham loved God and trusted that He had some reason to ask him to do such an awful thing. So, he took Isaac, without telling Sarah, and did not tell Isaac right away either. When they were nearing the place God had said, Isaac said, "Father, we have the wood for the fire, but where is the lamb?" Abraham replied, "Son, God will provide the lamb."

Eventually he had to explain to Isaac what God had told him to do. Isaac was old enough to tell his father off and refuse to comply with the whole seemingly wicked thing, but he loved and trusted his father, so agreed to allow his father to tie him up and put him on the altar they had prepared. Can you imagine how they both must have felt, with enormous pain and agony in both their hearts.

Abraham finally, with such emotion, raised the knife to kill his only son.

At that moment, the angel of the Lord shouted out, **"<ins>Abraham! Abraham! Lay not your hand upon the lad, neither do anything unto him: for now I know that you fear God, because you have not withheld your son, your only son, from me."</ins>**

Whew! Can you now imagine how Abraham and Isaac must have been so relieved and so thankful! Just then they heard the noise of a ram caught by its horns in a thicket, so they took the ram and offered it to God, instead of Isaac, Abraham's only son!

What a horrific but vivid illustration, of what our Heavenly Father, and His only begotten Son, had planned, before even Creation happened! **The only difference to Abraham and Isaac's experience, was that there was no one there to shout out, "Stop! Stop! Do not hurt or lay hands on your son!"**

Jesus, the only begotten Son, with a human mother, Mary, and His Father in Heaven as His Father, knew what was ahead of Him, and what the leaders of the Jewish people would do to Him.

Our loving God, **"Who speaks and it is done: Who commands and it stands fast."** (Psalm 33:9) could have wiped out that cruel crowd of leaders and the people who were following their leadership, **with just one Word**, but He refrained from destroying them because He loves His creation. He is not a God of **force** and is **"not willing that any should perish."** (2 Peter 3:9).

Please, stop and consider the scene. The people, **(who called themselves God's chosen people)**, were doing incredibly cruel things to Jesus throughout His arrest and trial. The whippings, the crown of thorns, the mocking and jeering, lead up to the tragic events on the hill of Calvary. Think about the terrible ache in both their hearts, especially our Heavenly Father as He watched what these wicked people were doing to His only begotten Son!

Think about the agony of the Father and His Son, as Jesus was carrying that heavy cross, with the people spitting on Him. Imagine the humiliation as the soldiers tore off His clothing, and lay Jesus down on the wooden cross. They stretched out His arms on that wooden cross, while they hammered sharp iron spikes through His hands and feet. Then they dropped that cross roughly into a hole in the rock, with a sign above His head saying, "King of the Jews."

What terrible ache in both their hearts as all this transpired. Why did the Omnipotent Creator, allow all this to happen, when with just one Word, it could all have been stopped!

He offers salvation to anyone who will **choose** to accept this enormous sacrifice, as payment in full for their sins. If we just **choose** to accept Jesus as Our Lord, our Creator and Redeemer, He offers us eternal life in an earth made new, where there will be no more sin, pain or death forever.

I really like that plan and am looking forward to seeing my Lord Jesus face to face and being able to thank him personally for His amazing love. My greatest wish and earnest prayer is that my loved ones, my children with their families, and many, many others will be there with me to thank Jesus also for offering them salvation from eternal death.

(You can read this whole story in the four Gospels and even in the Old Testament especially in Isaiah 53!)

Jesus didn't die from His crucifixion. He died from a broken heart. Some of His dying words were, **"Father, forgive them for they know not what they do!"** (Luke 23:34).

The Roman soldiers came to break all their legs and hurry their death so they couldn't breathe, because the Sabbath was drawing nigh. When they came to break Jesus' legs, He was already dead and they didn't need to break his legs, as they did to the two thieves! What incredible love displayed by our Heavenly Father and His only begotten Son, not just to us as earthly beings, but to all His created beings throughout His vast Universe.

What an incredible demonstration of our God Who is Love, providing a way for all men to be saved and receive forgiveness of sin, and have eternal life, if they would only **choose** to accept His loving gift of Salvation.

Jesus offered it to the thief on the cross, hanging on a cross beside Him, who called to Jesus for salvation, saying, **"Lord, remember me when You come into Your Kingdom!"**

Jesus replied, **"Verily, I say unto you this day, you shall be with Me in Paradise."** (Luke 23:42).

What a wonderful promise to the thief! When he witnessed Jesus' love, in spite of what that cruel hateful crowd were doing to Him, he realized that Jesus was indeed Who He claimed to be, **the promised Redeemer**!

He offers a place in His eternal Kingdom to <u>anyone</u> who <u>chooses</u> to accept Him as their Saviour and determines to walk with Jesus for the rest of his life! What amazing love God has for His creation!

It truly is, all about LOVE

CHAPTER 8

FOR THE LOVE OF A MAIDEN

Song of Solomon 8:6&7. This an interesting text, showing the strength of love from Solomon! **"Set me as a seal upon thine heart, as a seal upon thine arm: for love is strong as death; jealousy is cruel as the grave: the coals thereof are coals of fire, which have a most vehement flame. Many waters cannot quench love, neither can the floods drown it: if a man would give all the substance of his house for love, it would utterly be contemned."**

Of course, Solomon was thinking of marriage, and the love a man has for his bride, but it also applies to the love of God for His people, who choose to accept His wonderful gift of salvation.

I'd like to share with you now a little story of how much I was willing to go through for the love of my beautiful first wife, whose name was Ruth.

We spent sixty-one years together working for the Lord at home and over-seas, as missionary teachers, and before the Lord put her to sleep, peacefully, but unexpectedly. It was just before her eighty-first birthday. I was just like a lost sheep, before the Lord found another Godly companion for me, whose name was Naomi, and we were married in 2017, but that's another story!

My story below is one I have shared with my five children and friends years ago:

FOR THE LOVE OF A MAIDEN.

It was first term-end break at the Queensland Teachers' College, and I hadn't seen my special girl for some months. She was living and working at The Plateau on her grandparent's farm near Mulgildie, not far from Monto. It was a large farm, with very red volcanic soil, and they grew corn and peanuts in rotation.

In May we had been having some very heavy rains for some time and the rivers and creeks were flooding. I had a Matchless 500 motorcycle, and my plan was to travel from Brisbane to the farm which normally would be about a four hour run, to spend some time with my beloved before I had to return to Brisbane to start the next semester at Teachers' College.

With just a few essentials in my knapsack I set off about 9am. It was quite cold and wet, so I had leather gloves on my hands, and a raincoat worn back to front to hopefully keep out the rain. My hands soon seemed like ice even inside the gloves. Motorcycles are miserable things to travel on in cold wet weather, but I had a very compelling reason to keep going.

I had only made progress a little north of Ipswich when I was blocked by the first river crossing which was well over the road bridge, with lots of cars on both sides just waiting for the waters to subside. I was not in the mood to wait for hours so started looking around for some other way to continue my journey. Aha!

Not more than a few hundred metres upstream, I spied a railway bridge, and somehow, I managed to get the bike through the fence into the cattle paddock and set off through the long grass towards the railway line. About three quarters of the way through, the bike hit a log and threw me off into the wet grass. I managed to stand the bike up again and continued to the railway fence. With a lot of effort, I managed to get through the fence just as a train went by. Another aha!

There shouldn't be any more trains for a while, so up onto the rail line and bumpity-bump across the sleepers and across the bridge safely with the nasty river raging by below, snarling at my successful crossing. Not far along the rail line north, I spied a dirt road running parallel to the rail line, so again with great difficulty, I manoeuvred the bike through the fence, by laying it down on its side and dragging it under the bottom wire. It was much more comfortable on the road instead of bumping along over the rail sleepers.

The rain began pouring down in earnest, but I was able to connect up soon with the main road and arrived at Goomeri about nightfall. I had no tent so just lay down beside my bike in the local park and tried to get some sleep wrapped in my raincoat. The rain and cold made it very nasty, and after a little rest I decided to continue my journey. All went well but travel was very slow because of the rain and road conditions. As I was nearing Monto, the main road was completely and deeply submerged at one place, but I met a local chap who knew another way round the water, and so I followed him.

It was somewhere near Three Moon Creek, and at one place it looked like a sea of water a few hundred metres across. The chap in the car got through alright, so I decided to follow even though the water was almost a foot deep. My faithful bike never missed a beat, but sounded like a speed boat, as the exhaust gases exited under water, with that muffled gurgling, gurgling sound.

I was able to continue without further problems until I arrived at the farm gate. It was still raining and about 2am in the morning. That red soil and water mix was something I had not counted on. I had not travelled a few metres when the bike just refused to stay upright because the road was so slippery. I tried numerous things to keep it going, but the wheels had now become clogged with the red mud and refused to turn, so I just leaned it up against a fence post and continued the last kilometre or so on foot. Even on foot I had trouble keeping upright.

What a relief to finally arrive at the farmhouse, but at 2am in the morning I was reluctant to wake everyone up, so had a guess at where my darling might be sleeping, and very gently knocked on the wall, calling her name softly. Success! She heard me, and soon I had her in my arms on the back veranda.

After changing into some warm dry clothes, we talked for an hour or more and then I thankfully bedded down on the veranda couch for the rest of the night.

It's amazing what a young man in love will do to be with his beloved. What a drama to travel in such weather, with floods and rain on just a motorcycle.

Was it all worth it? You bet!

We married in 1956, and were still together, and very happy nearly sixty years "down the track", till 2016 when the Lord put her to sleep very peacefully, but unexpectedly, just before her 81st birthday, and after over sixty years together, walking and working for the Lord at Home and Abroad.

Ruth was my Princess and will always have a special place in my heart!

Before she passed away, **Ruth** told me a few times that if she should die before me, that I should ask the Lord to find another Godly companion. He certainly did do that for me and in 2017 I found **Naomi**, who had been a widow for nineteen years, and that's another incredible story which again demonstrates our Heavenly Father's character.

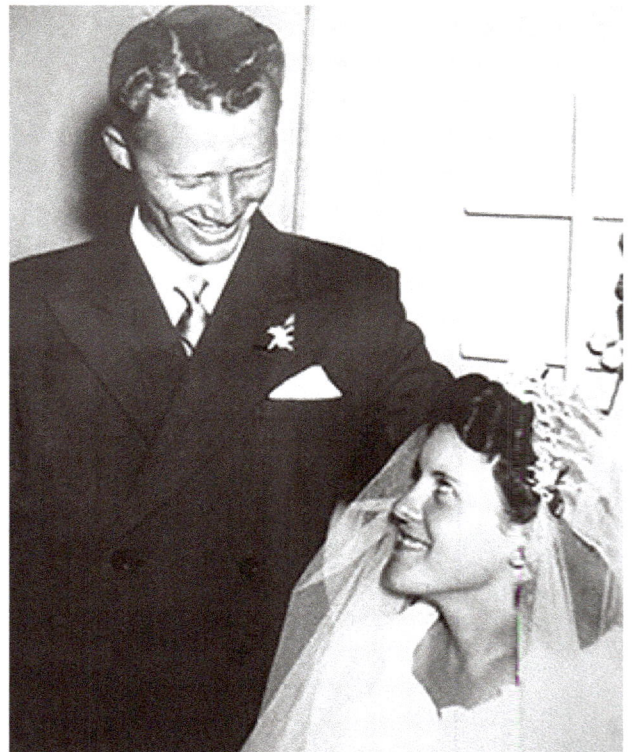

He truly is my loving Heavenly Father!   It's all about LOVE!

CHAPTER 9

NOTHING IS IMPOSSIBLE WITH GOD

When my wife of sixty years passed away unexpectedly but very peacefully in 2016, life for me became suddenly very lonely and empty indeed, as we were seldom ever apart and did nearly everything together. We met at Avondale College in 1953 and had been together for nearly sixty-three years in total. **Ruth was my Princess** and will always occupy a large portion of my heart and memories.

I was caring for the home of some good friends near my daughter Jennelle at Camden at the end of 2016. I believe it was Jennelle who said to me one day when I was feeling exceptionally lonely, **"Dad, why don't you have a look on the internet for a companion?"**

"Don't be ridiculous!" I replied. **"You don't find a Godly companion on the internet!"**

However, out of real loneliness, curiosity and serious prayer, I felt impressed to have a look at a site called **Christian Connection.** There were some interesting ladies' profiled there, but none even came close to my lifestyle as a Vegan and an unchurched individual whose only rule of life and understanding of Truth, was based solely on the Word of God.

I was about to give up and told the Lord that I would probably have to live the rest of my life on my own, when I noticed **Naomi**. Hmmm!

When I started to read her profile that she had placed there, a very definite feeling of peace and yet excitement came over me. I continued reading and was so amazed at the similarities that we both shared. In the Bible story of Gideon God gave him two definite signs. There were over twenty signs He gave me about Naomi and the list just kept growing daily as we communicated with each other. I'll list some below which were really amazing:

1. **Love for God and His Truth is supreme for us both.**

2. **Naomi and Ruth**. In the Bible story Ruth says, **"Entreat me not to leave you, or to turn from following after you; where you go I will go; where you lodge I will lodge; your God will be my God."** Two wonderful ladies who really loved God and put Him first in everything. When Ruth and I were married we became united as one couple in the Lord. It was as if she was speaking to Naomi on my behalf.

3. **We both have had five wonderful children**, who are still alive and love us.

4. **Naomi had been a widow for nineteen years and I was a widower for just months**. Neither of us have been tangled up in divorce or been involved with any other person as a couple.

5. **Music.** We both play piano and other instruments. We love music and praising the Lord in song. Naomi also loves Messianic Dancing and has taught me one already with more to come. The dances express the Gospel message very beautifully.

6. **We are both Sabbath-keepers**, and revere His special Day, the seventh day, and the rest of the commandments as well of course. This was very important for me, as I had kept the seventh-day Sabbath my whole life.

7. **Neither of us are members of any church organization**, but we both love the Lord Jesus with all our hearts and minds. We both enjoy the freedom to follow the Holy Spirit's leading as we consider Present Truth from His Word, as our Chart and Compass. We both believe God has His faithful remnant in all the churches and He excludes no one. It is an open invitation for "Whosoever will, may come."

8. **We both recognize that God used Ellen White** to counsel His people, and that she was given special messages for those who live at the end of time.

9. **Our understanding of Life After Death is based solely on the Word of God.** There is no eternally burning hell, and we simply rest as if fast asleep till the Redeemer calls forth His saints at His second coming. We both are looking forward to the Resurrection Day, to seeing my Princess raised from sleep, and Naomi's Tom be restored to life with glorious new bodies. What a day that will be!

10. **We both have a keen interest in God's way of keeping healthy in body, mind and spirit.**

11. **We were both christened as babies in the Anglican Church.** I still have my certificate!

12. **We both had a desire to work for God at a very young age.**

13. **Naomi doesn't have "dingles and dangles", expensive jewellery or tattoos.** Her character and love for God is her beauty. The Lord tells us specifically not to cut our bodies for decoration or make marks in our flesh. Leviticus 19:28. Perhaps a plain wedding ring would be OK, especially today in modern countries where it shows all around that we are married. Ruth used to wear one.

14. **We both are heavily waiting on the Lord for His leading**, and we believe He definitely is leading in all aspects of our lives.

15. **We both have majored in English**, and love reading and writing, and have written our life stories in little booklets as Autobiographies. There'll have to be new chapters written soon I believe.

16. **We both understand the correct view on Baptism into Christ**, rather than into a particular denomination.

17. **Fruit for breakfast seems to suit us both**. It certainly does fit in with the body's Circadian Rhythms, and we both believe in caring for our body temples.

18. **We both are outgoing and love meeting and working with people.**

19. **We both were looking forward to the possibility of sharing life with another Godly companion.**

20. **Even our vehicles had travelled nearly the same mileage!** Amazing!

And the list grows exponentially as time passes.......

I asked if I could call her on the phone, while I was house caring at Camden, and it was awesome to speak to each other realizing that we were both leading very similar lives with the Lord as our Anchor and Counsellor. So, I asked if we could meet, and we had a lovely day together at her place at Glenbrook sharing our goals and understandings of truth.

After that visit, we emailed and exchanged messages and calls, getting to know as much as possible about each other.

I personally have been amazed repeatedly, at how the Lord is leading us both, so I told Naomi I'd like to drive down from Ellesmere near Kingaroy, my home base on my daughter's property, to spend a few weeks near her to find out more if our coming together would be possible.

It's about sixteen hours driving, but I arrived safely, and she told me she'd like me to stay at her apartment as she had a separate space for me to have privacy, and that was so lovely of her.

It was Thursday evening when I arrived, and we chatted till late into the night, and then retired. On Sabbath we met the folks at the Seventh-Day Baptist venue near Parramatta and I got to know some of those dear people. On Sunday the family were to have a "get together" at Katoomba for Heiko's birthday, and it would be a great time to meet some of the family members who live in the Sydney area.

I was still amazed that the Lord had found another Godly woman who could be a companion for me so quickly after Ruth's passing, for whatever time I have left to live for Him. Linking up with another lady was a really huge undertaking for me, and I wanted to be absolutely sure that the Lord wanted to see me ask Naomi to marry me. So, I spent a great deal of time with the Lord in prayer on the Saturday evening. It had been raining almost continuously since I had arrived, and so I made a pact with the Lord. If He dispersed the clouds and stopped the rain and allowed the sun to shine fully on the Three Sisters near Katoomba, I would take that as a special sign to go ahead.

Well, at 2pm it was still clouded over and raining, and I was wondering if after all the other signs and similarities, that He was going to say "No!" But the rain did ease off enough for us to go for a walk with the family, and the clouds were clearing, so we said our "Goodbyes" and drove off to see the Three Sisters.

By the time we arrived, the sun had emerged and was shining in full strength on those three rock formations as in the picture below.

My heart was so full and overflowing with gratitude to my Lord. As we gazed upon the beautiful sight, I told Naomi that these rock formations were misnamed. The tall One on the left was really Yahweh; the middle one was Don, and the smaller one was Naomi.

Then I took Naomi's hand and asked her to be my wife and …………she said,

"YES"!

I told Naomi of the pact I had made with the Lord. We hugged and kissed and were both overcome with the excitement of another amazing and direct answer to prayer.

Ecclesiastes 4:12 says, "A three-fold cord is not quickly broken." We felt so grateful to our Heavenly Father Who is indeed the strong unbreakable strand in our cord.

I had brought my camera with me, and wondered how I could get some pictures of this very special occasion, when I noticed two ladies walking towards us. As I approached, and before I had a chance to speak, one lady said,

"Would you like me to take some pictures for you?"

I told them what had just happened, and they were nearly as excited as we were. They took some lovely pictures of us both, and I'll include a couple below, as a memorial of this wonderful occasion. What a wonderful Father we serve!

What overwhelming LOVE He has for His children!

CHAPTER 10

THE TWO EMPIRES

There are two empires in our world. One has Lucifer, the Serpent, Satan, the great Deceiver, and his followers in charge, determined to take control of our world here on earth, and the other one is **God's empire ruled by the Omnipotent, Omniscient, and Omnipresent Heavenly Father, the Great I AM, His only begotten Son, Jesus Christ, and God's Holy Spirit!**

For about 6000 years on earth, these two empires have been at war! One is using **Force**, and the other is based on **LOVE**!

Why is this war still going on? One writer has written a book called **"The Great Controversy"** which describes the conflict in detail from begining to end. It is very obvious to me that our God, Who is **LOVE**, and Who is not willing that any should perish, is still giving everyone the opportunity to see His love, and accept the wonderful free gift of salvation that He is offering to us all. Because He is a God of **Love** and not a God of **Force, He is allowing this whole battle to continue for a <u>predetermined time</u>.**

However, He has a plan in place, clearly outlined in His Word. He shows it all clearly in His Word, and in this amazing prophecy of Daniel 2. It is an offer to be repentant of our sins, and, of our own free will, to **choose** to accept His totally free offer; to **choose** His empire, accepting His offer of salvation and eternal life in an earth made new. As this world becomes more and more wicked, He shows us what is surely coming, and when He says: **"Enough! My offer is no longer available!"** it will be too late to be part of His Kingdom!

He has made known through His Prophets what shall be the end of this whole war that has been going on for about six thousand years, here on earth.

Now I would like to share some most amazing prophecies, that clearly show that the time of probation is about to close.

In the book of Daniel Chapter Two, the then ruler of the world was a fellow called Nebuchadnezzer, who gained his authority by force.

One night he had a vision of a great statue with a head of pure **Gold**; it's chest was made of **Silver;** it's belly and thighs were made of **Brass**; it's legs were made of **Iron**, and the feet were made of a mixture of **Iron and Clay.** Then he saw a **great Stone** cut out without hands, which came down and smashed the image on the feet, breaking it all to tiny pieces. **That Stone increased in size, and filled the whole earth and there were no more images after this!**

Well, Nebuchadnezzer was very troubled over this dream but he couldn't remember it all. So, he called all his wise men, magicians, fortune-tellers and sorcerers, and told them to tell him what he had dreamed, and explain what it all meant.

They said, "Tell us the dream and we will show you the meaning."

The king said that if they couldn't tell him the dream, he would have them all put to death.

When God's man, Daniel, and his three Hebrew friends, who were taken captive, and also considered some of the wise men, heard about the king's command, they went to prayer, and asked God to show them the dream and it's meaning.

God showed Daniel the dream and it's meaning. So, he asked for an audience with the King and told him what he had dreamed and what it all meant.

You can read all about it in the book of **Daniel Chapter Two.**

The king saw a great image, as described above. A picture of it as it may have been is as below, with all the different metals and the mixture of iron and clay in the feet, and the great stone smashing it all to bits and filling the whole earth, with nothing more to follow!

Nebuchadnezzar was not pleased that there would be other kingdoms to follow his kingdom, so he had an image wholly made of just pure gold, and commanded all in his kingdom to bow down to this image of himself. If anyone **chose** not to bow down, they would be cast into a burning fiery furnace. Three Hebrew men, Shadrach, Meshack and Abednego, who worhipped only the true God, remained standing. What happened next you can read about for yourself in the book of Daniel 3: 1-20. It is a fascinating record, and another demonstration of God's love for those who **choose** to follow His laws of love. They **chose** to follow the second of God's Ten Commandments:

"Thou shalt not make unto thee any graven image, or any likeness of anything that is in heaven above, or that is in the earth beneath, or that is in the water under the earth: Thou shalt not bow down thyself to them, nor serve them."

How God saved these men who were faithful to Him, is truly another demonstration of His love for His people! The story is all recorded in Daniel Chapter 3.

In Daniel chapter 2, we have a prophecy that shows the history of the world right up to our time. God showed King Nebuchadnezzar an amazing dream which none of his "wise men" could explain. Eventually God showed Daniel the dream and what it meant. It is a fascinating story told in full in chapter 2 of Daniel's book.

All of this dream has come about if you care to check with the history of the world, and various rulers trying to take over the world, as men are trying to do today through the New World Order, United Nations, and the World Economic Forum. We are surely in the time of the feet of Iron and Clay. It is very near the time when the great Stone, cut out without hands, will be God's eternal kingdom, where only Love for our wonderful God will rule!

In the picture we see the kingdom of **Babylon** which was ruled by Nebuchadnezzar, who was the head of **Gold**.

The breast of **Silver** was the kingdom of **Medo-Persia**, with Cyrus the Great as ruler.

Next was the **Brass** kingdom of **Greece** with Alexander the Great in charge.

Then came the **Iron** kingdom of **Rome** with firstly, Julius Caesar in charge, till he was murdered and other rulers followed, right to the time of Christ.

You can check all of this history in any good library.

Nebuchadnezzar's Dream of The Latter Days

BABYLON
606-538 BC
"This image's head was of fine gold... Thou art this head of gold." (Daniel 2: 32, 38).

PERSIA
538-331 BC
"...His breast and his arms of silver... after thee shall arise another Kingdom inferior to thee..." (Daniel 2:32, 39).

GREECE
331-63 BC
"...His belly and his thighs of brass... another third Kingdom of brass, which shall bear rule over all the earth." (Daniel 2: 32, 39).

ROME
27 BC-
1453 AD
"His legs of Iron...And the fourth Kingdom shall be strong as Iron: for as much as Iron breaketh in pieces and subdueth all things.: " (Daniel 2:33, 40).

DIVIDED
ROMAN EMPIRE
WRE 27 BC-476 AD
ERE 67 AD-1453 AD
" His feet part of Iron and part of clay... partly strong and partly broken... they shall not cleave one to another." (Daniel 2:33, 41-43).

CHRIST'S
KINGDOM
"...A stone...smote the Image upon his feet...(and) became a mountain, and filled the whole earth... the God of heaven (shall) set up a Kingdom, which shall never be destroyed.... " (Daniel 2:34, 35, 44).

Any honest person can see that we are today in the time of the kingdoms of **Iron mixed with Clay**; **strong nations and weak nations** calling themselves, the **New World Order, United Nations** and so on, with mega-rich men trying to rule the world.

Why has God showed us all this? It is so that we can see that His Word, the Scriptures, the Bible, is true! Again, **He is not willing that any should perish**. He is comparing the efforts of men guided by the enemy of God, the Devil, Lucifer, Satan, ruling by Force, with God's Kingdom of Love.

It is an amazing, and very loving plan to show clearly the difference between LOVE and FORCE.

His arms are wide open to receive even the worst of sinners. While Jesus was here on earth, He fellowshipped with tax collectors, prostitutes, thieves, demon possessed and healed the sick and needy. He even raised Lazarus and Jairus' daughter from the dead!

What a wonderful loving God we have Who has an empire built on **LOVE** instead of **FORCE**! In God's eternal kingdom, "**The lion shall eat straw like the ox.**" Isaiah 11: 6-9

It's all about love! Hmmm!

CHAPTER 11

TRUE AUSTRALIAN STORY

Most of the people of this world today are not aware of what is ahead for our sad old earth. They are ignorant regarding God's clear warnings that His probationary period is about to come to an end. The general theme seems to be chasing houses and lands, enjoying all sorts of sports and pleasures, with crime increasing at an alarming rate.

Our children are being taught that the human species just evolved by accident from a "Big Bang", billions of years ago, and gradually developing from some slime out of a swamp to lower forms of life such as insects, small creatures like rats and mice, to higher forms like birds, fish and animals, including monkeys and apes, which then developed over billions of years into humans like we have today. Hmm! I dealt with this incredible hypothesis, in Chapter 2.

Is it any wonder that there is so much juvenile crime and other crimes happening and reported every night on the news?

When we reject God, we reject the Laws He put in place, showing us how to live. The laws of the jungle then become the norm as we see so often today, with young people, and older people, committing all sorts of horrible crimes, and many nations and religious factions fighting each other, persecuting and killing innocent men, women and children. That's not **Love**! It is **Force**, the very opposite of God's laws of **Love**!

I'd like now to share a story called **"True Australian Story"** which graphically illustrates how Satan has deceived the human race.

Jesus says in Matthew 24:44, **"Therefore be ye also ready: for in such an hour as ye think not the Son of man cometh"**.

TRUE AUSTRALIAN STORY

The Tasmanian Wolf, (now extinct), in the early days of settlement in Tasmania, enjoyed fresh mutton, and was causing considerable loss to the farmers' flocks of sheep and lambs. So, the farmers arranged a day to chase the Wolf with their hounds. They started very early in the morning, and the hounds soon picked up the scent near a creek and the chase was on. The hounds were away and the farmers following on horseback like the old English "fox and hounds" hunt.

As the chase proceeded the farmers caught occasional glimpses of the Wolf. He was well ahead of the hounds and was heading for the mountains. The way soon became too steep for the horses, so the farmers waited in the valley below, and watched with binoculars. Now and then they saw the Wolf winding its way to the top of a ridge, along to a part where there was a sheer cliff at least three hundred feet high. It looked like the Wolf would be trapped as it came to very edge of the cliff, but then they watched as the Wolf did something very strange. The Wolf carefully turned around, and quickly retraced his steps to a large rock beside the trail, jumped quickly aside and lay down on

37

the cliff side of the large rock. It was not long of course, before the hounds came bounding along past the rock, noses to the ground, full speed ahead on the hot scent, slightly uphill. The farmers were aghast! They fired their guns and shouted loudly, but to no avail. They watched helplessly as their prized hunting dogs went over the cliff, one by one, and hurtled to their death on the rocks three hundred feet below! When all was quiet, they watched as the Wolf leisurely rose, ambled up to the edge of the cliff, surveyed the carnage below, and then turned and calmly went on his way.

This story for me, graphically illustrates how Satan works, setting traps for the unwary. This old world is racing to its close, noses to the ground, chasing dollars, houses, lands, investments, sports and cares of this life, unaware that just ahead is eternal death for all who neglect to study the whole scene, and who fail to hear the warnings shouted to us from the Scriptures.

We are very near the end of the trail for this world. God is shouting to us to watch and see the signs and warnings He has given in His Word. In His love, He is calling, nay shouting, **"STOP! Watch out! There is danger ahead!"** Look up and view the whole scene. Get your noses off the earth. Use the binoculars provided for us all in the Word of God. It is called Prophecy and also Jesus' own words. **The Bible tells us plainly of the signs that show us we are very near the "cliff edge".**

Check out the words of Jesus in Matthew 24 when He answers His disciple's question as to when the end of the world would occur. Check out also Daniel chapter 7 to 12. Also, the Gospel of Luke, chapter 21. Go to Revelation 11, 12 and 13 for more details that show that His coming is near. The Bible tells us plainly of the signs that show us we are very near the "cliff edge. **BE READY!**

All the Bible Prophecies have proven true. Just look at the Daniel 2 prophecy. Every kingdom portrayed has come and gone and we are right now situated in the iron and clay of the feet and toes.

The very next event is the great stone, cut out without hands. It smashes the image on the feet and grows into a great mountain filling the whole earth, and no more kingdoms follow this event. It is the Kingdom of God which stands forever.

I want to be part of that kingdom, with no more sin, suffering or death for eternity, living with my Saviour Jesus forever! **Oh, how great is His love!** He's **"not willing that anyone should perish**! 2 Peter 3:9

Won't you join with me to be there in God's Eternal Kingdom?

Our love for our Saviour and Lord grows stronger as we get to know Him.

CHAPTER 12

SEVENTY WEEKS OF YEARS

In God's amazing Book is another incredible prophecy which again shows how accurate and truthful is God's Book, the Bible! It is found in Daniel Chapter 9: 21-27. Daniel had been praying earnestly for understanding, as to why the Jewish people were suffering slavery. In verse 21 the angel Gabriel was sent by the Lord to help Daniel understand. In verse 24 the prophecy of the angel Gabriel begins:

"Seventy weeks are determined upon thy people, and on thy holy city; to finish the transgression; and to make an end of sins; and to make reconciliation for iniquity; and to bring in everlasting righteousness; and to seal up the vision and prophecy; <u>and to anoint the most holy.</u> (Sprinkling of the blood of the Lamb on the Mercy Seat.)

Know therefore and understand, that from the going forth of the commandment to restore and to build Jerusalem, unto Messiah, the Prince, shall be seven weeks, and three score and two weeks; the street shall be built again, and the wall even in troublous times.

And after three score and two weeks shall Messiah be cut off, but not for himself: and the people of the prince that shall come, shall destroy the city and the sanctuary; and the end thereof shall be with a flood, and unto the end of the war, desolations are determined.

And he shall confirm the covenant with many for one week: and in the midst of the week, he shall cause the sacrifice and oblation to cease, and for the overspreading of abominations he shall make it desolate, even until the consummation and that determined shall be poured upon the desolate."

This prophecy has a double application. One is about the rejection of the Jewish people, as His chosen people, and the destruction of Jerusalem. The other application is to do with the end of this world, and the setting up of God's eternal Kingdom.

Everything in this prophecy could not be accomplished in just seventy literal weeks, so the Lord is clearly speaking of **seventy weeks of years.** That's seventy times seven which is four hundred and ninety years, and that's exactly how it all happened. History shows clearly the details exactly.

The going forth of the commandment to restore and rebuild Jerusalem was a decree by Artaxerxes in 457 BC.

After the first week of seven years, Jerusalem was rebuilt with its wall in very troublous times. After that there were sixty-two weeks of years to when Jesus was baptised by John in the Jordan, in **27AD**, and began His ministry.

(AD is "Anno Domini", the year of the Great Teacher.)

27AD was the start of the final week of Gabriel's prophecy.

In the midst of this final week, Jesus was crucified on Calvary's hill, and **"caused the sacrifice and offering to cease."** That was AD 31!

When the thick curtain before the Most Holy Place, was torn from top to bottom, no doubt with a loud noise, **at exactly three o'clock in our time**, it revealed an empty room with no Ark there!

I can imagine how the priest was so shocked that he dropped the knife, and the little lamb ran away! The real Lamb of God was offered and died on Calvary's cross, **at that precise hour!**

So ended forever, the sacrificial services, because the **type** had met **anti-type**. The price for our sins was **PAID FOR IN FULL!** This showed how true is God's Word, all predicted in the prophecy of Daniel 9 and fulfilled exactly.

It all occurred exactly, at the very **YEAR** at the end of the 62 weeks of years, in the midst of the last week, in 31AD. at the very **MONTH** of Nissan, the time of the Passover, at the very **DAY** of the month, the fourteenth day, and even at the very **HOUR** of the evening sacrifice.

How precisely fulfilled is this prophecy! The <u>year</u>, the <u>month</u>, the <u>day</u>, and even the <u>hour</u>!

How incredible a fulfilment of this amazing prophecy! How exact is God's Holy Word!

But that's not the end of this amazing prophecy. Jesus, the Lamb of God, was crucified in the <u>midst</u> of that last week, three and a half years from when John baptized Him in the Jordan. There were still three and a half years to go to the end of that last week!

What happened at the end of that three and half years after Jesus' death in the midst of the week? There were still three and a half years for the Jewish people, to accept the sacrifice of Jesus, as the Messiah, the true Lamb of God, and to embrace the amazing love of God!

Sadly, most of the Jewish people still rejected God's amazing offer. In 34AD, which completed the seventy weeks of years, the disciple Stephen, was sharing the whole story of Jesus' life and ministry as the promised Messiah, with a crowd of Jewish people. They became so angry with Stephen that they took up stones, and stoned him to death, thus rejecting their last opportunity of salvation as a nation.

That was the end of the seventy weeks of years of Daniel 9.

As the disciples continued to preach the Gospel story, many Jewish people did accept Jesus as the Messiah, the Lamb of God. Many Jewish people today have accepted Jesus as their Saviour and Lord.

God is no respecter of persons. **"He is not willing that any should perish".** 2Peter 3:9

Jews and Gentiles can join together, **"as the branch is grafted to the vine".** Romans 11:11-31

No matter who we are, if we **choose** to accept **God's Love,** we can have our names inscribed in the Lamb's Book of Life!

"If we are Christ's, then are we Abraham's seed and heirs according to the promise!" Galatians 3:29. How wonderful is our loving God!

Jews and gentiles can join together, "as the branch is connected to the vine." Romans11: 11-31

RACES OF MANKIND

MONGOLIAN	CAUCASIAN	MALAY	AMERICAN	ETHIOPIAN
1 Tungoos Woman 2 Kirghiz	7 Cossack 8 Georgian Woman 9 Carlmerlan	15 Dink Woman 16 Malay Woman	21 Eskimo (Labrador) 22 Sioux (No. Amer.) 23 Masai	29 Zulu 30 Loango
4 Canton Woman 4 Korean	10 Persian 11 Arab 12 Swede	17 Andaman Islander 18 Samoan Woman	23 Apache (No. Amer.) 24 Mexican Squaw 31 Abyssinian	32 Nubian 33 Bushman
5 Japanese Woman 6 Tchuktchi	13 Scotchman 14 Italian (Sicily)	19 Fijian 20 Maori	25 Botuto (Brazil) 26 Araucanian (Chile)	
			27 Fuegian Woman	

Again, it is a demonstration of God's love for all mankind regardless of colour or creed!

CHAPTER 13

INCREASE OF KNOWLEDGE AND RUNNING TO AND FRO

Following on from the chapter, the True Australian Story, we see another amazing fulfilment of prophecy. Another effort by our loving God to show us the "cliff" is just ahead. Look up and view the whole scene. Use the binoculars provided for us all in the Word of God. It is called Prophecy. The Bible tells us plainly of the signs that show us we are very near the "**cliff edge**".

In the book of Daniel, chapter 12 and verse 4, after the Lord gave Daniel a number of visions of the end times, God says,

"But thou, O Daniel, shut up the words and seal the book, even to "the time of the end": <u>many shall run to and fro, and knowledge shall be increased."</u>

For approximately six thousand years, men have travelled on foot, or by animal drawn carriages, or on horseback. Sea travel has been by sailing ships, and there was no air travel till just before my day. For six thousand years, weapons of war have been bows and arrows, spears, and swords. For six thousand years men have carried on the way of life from ancient times, planting by hand, harvesting by hand, without any significant change, but just in my short lifetime of eighty-nine years now, in 2024, rapid change has happened so quickly, fulfilling the Scripture that **"many shall run to and fro, and knowledge shall be increased."**

Just in my lifetime, sailing ships were the only means for inter-continental travel.

Now we have huge Cruise Liners travelling the world, carrying huge numbers of passengers, with many decks, ensuites for First Class passengers, huge kitchens, and every modern convenience on board. There are even heated swimming pools on board and every kind of pleasures for entertainment!

Just in my lifetime!

What about <u>Flight</u>?

Not long before I was born, in 1903, the Wright Brothers, Orville and Wilbur, had made the first flying machine! <u>Their longest trial flight was one minute!</u> Now, **<u>just in my lifetime</u>**, we have so many different aircraft, satellites, submarines, helicopters, and huge Airbuses that have two or three decks carrying six hundred or more passengers. On the upper deck for First Class people, are several cabins with full ensuites. There is a kitchen providing all sorts of meals, as the aircraft travels from one side of the world to the other in just several hours!

Four large Rolls Royce engines create such power, to lift this huge machine, weighing many tons into the air at tremendous speeds.

Thousands of gallons of fuel are pumped into its fuel tanks to provide energy for this amazing machine!

I wonder what the pioneers of flight, the Wright Brothers, would say if they could see these huge flying machines?

Just in my lifetime, we have so many different means of **Communication**. There are now amazing computers, laptops for all trading, financial deals, records of all kinds, photographing, even videos.

Nearly everyone, including children, have a small hand-held mobile phone today. They can play all sorts of weird and wonderful games. Wherever we go they can direct your travel, play all sorts of music and we only need to speak to it to find anything we need to know in seconds! It even can tell us Scripture references of any verse or subject in God's Word!

Just in my lifetime, we now have television devices with large screens to listen to all sorts of programmes, movies, sermons, news and on and on!

When we came home from New Guinea where my wife and I, and our five children spent eleven years in mission service, we saw these TVs, as they are called. My children kept pestering us to get one for our home, where I was posted as Headmaster of the church school in Mullumbimby.

There was a second-hand shop in Mullumbimby run by a friend who agreed to let me have a TV set to try it out.

Well, it wasn't long before we were eating our meals in front of this amazing device, the chores were piling up, the children's homework was being neglected, and so I returned the thing to my friend's shop! My children were very cross with me, but we were able to return to some sort of normality!

Just in my lifetime, we have incredible increase in knowledge in the **Medical Field!** Transplants of organs, including hearts, from dying donors, artificial joints can be inserted, drugs to treat every kind of malady. How amazing is medical science today.

Just in my lifetime, we have **Space Travel** and satellites, space stations, drones, and even men on the moon. We have submarines which can travel round the world underwater without surfacing! Many of these cost billions of dollars to build and are equipped with all sorts of modern weaponry, including nuclear weapons, which if used, can wipe out whole cities. This happened to end World War 2, in 1945, by destroying the Japanese cities of Nagasaki and Hiroshima with one atomic bomb!

Just in my lifetime, we have trains run by **Electricity**. Thousands of vehicles travel on highways at incredible speeds every day. The highways have to be continually upgraded to more and more lanes, to cope with the daily increase of "**men running to and fro**". Trucks and buses, motorcycles, and cars of many types made by companies all over the world. My wife and I even have a modern vehicle, which has all sorts of modern gadgets. Phones that can make or answer calls at the touch of a button on the steering wheel; screens with all sorts of menus that boggle the mind; cameras fitted to front and rear with results that can be seen on the screen!

Just in my lifetime, there are **Machines** that can do so many jobs that used to be done by hand!

When I was just sixteen years old, the sugar cane was cut by hand with a cane knife, then it was loaded by hand on to cane trucks for the mill. I was carting those cane trucks out of the paddock with a wagon and three draught horses. Now, a machine does the whole process while the driver sits in his air-conditioned cab listening to his favourite music, with a truck and driver beside him, with its driver also in an air-conditioned cab with his radio or music, as the first machine loads the cut cane onto his truck for the mill. What incredible **"increase in knowledge"**, <u>**just in my lifetime!**</u>

There are Cranes to lift incredible weights, and Bulldozers to build huge dams and move huge amounts of soils and rocks, and on and on!

All these things are fulfilling the prophecies of Daniel in chapter 12, and the signs Jesus Himself gave us in Mathew 24, Mark 13, and Luke 21. Daniel's prophecies from chapter 7 to 12 speak of the **"time of the end"**, <u>nearly ten times,</u> when <u>**knowledge shall be increased, and men shall run to and fro."**</u>

Well, that's just the <u>beginning</u> of the "increase in knowledge" just in my lifetime! Let's have a closer look at more of this amazing **increase of knowledge, and men running to and fro, <u>just in my lifetime!</u>**

Computers can store incredible amounts of data with all sorts of "Apps" for any requirements! Almost all buying and selling, banking and transfers of funds, is controlled and made available to everyone by computers!

Woolworths, for example, send us "specials", on the usual items of foods or other items that we normally purchase. Cash buying and selling is becoming a thing of the past. Now we all have Credit and Debit Cards that we just touch on a small machine, and it is all done and recorded on your receipt. On one occasion, a boy of about twelve years old was in front of us at the "checkout", at "Fresh and Save", and we watched him just put his hand on this small machine to pay for his goods, took his receipt and walked out with his purchases. Somehow, he had an identity mark on his hand to do the transaction! We were shocked to watch this happen before our eyes! It reminded us of the Scripture in Revelation 11, that unless we have a special mark in our hands or forehead, we will not be allowed to buy or sell! There's even face recognition now that can do likewise!

Here are a few pictures of when I was a boy growing up, and what it is like now, in 2024, and it has all happened so quickly fulfilling the prophecy of **the time of the end** of Daniel 12:4. again proving the truth of God's Word. In Daniel's book in chapters 7 to 12, **the time of the end** is spoken about ten times or so. What we are seeing today, are the signs that our loving God has given us who are surely living in the **TIME OF THE END**. This world as it is, is about to end, and we need to be ready as much as we can and help others also to realise that there is a **Cliff Face** not far ahead, as in the **True Australian Story**.

Let's not be like the people of Noah's day. They were eating and drinking, marrying and giving in marriage, **"noses on the ground"**, searching for the things of earth; houses, lands, money, sports and pleasures of all kinds, till the flood came and took them all away! Matthew 24:38.

Here are some pictures of what I have seen, of what it was like as I grew up, to what it is like today! After 6000 years of primitive living, life has changed so suddenly, **just in my lifetime of nearly 90 years.** Surely that is proof of the prophecy of Daniel 12 where God says: In the last days, the time of the end, **"Knowledge shall be increased, and men shall run to and fro."** Daniel 12:4

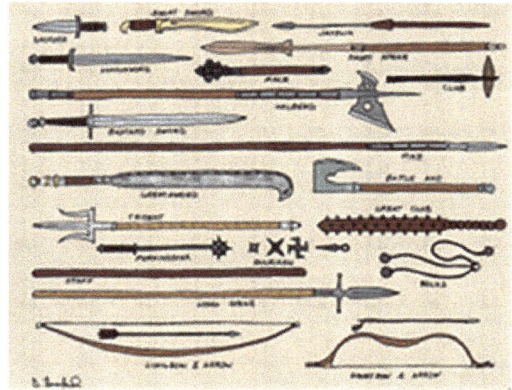

Just in my lifetime of nearly 90 years, in 2024, from Horse and Buggy, Ancient weapons, first Mobile phones, the Outhouse, ("dunny"), only Sailing Ships for International Travel to what we have today……

When I was just 16, I was cutting sugar cane by hand with a cane-knife. **"Stoop, chop: straighten top"**! Then I had to load it onto wagons by hand, and cart it out of the paddock, for the locomotive to take it to the mill, **with three draft horses!**

Now we have huge machines doing the whole lot, with the operator enjoying an air-conditioned cab, listening to his favourite music!

Now today, we see such incredible changes, in nearly every area of human life, **"JUST IN MY LIFETIME"** that it "blows my mind" when I think of the incredible **"increase of knowledge and men running to and fro."**

Please pardon me for repeating myself. Our loving Heavenly Father has given us so many signs, and warnings that we are truly **nearing the edge of the cliff**, where this sad, sin-sick world is about to end, and the time we have left to accept His gracious and merciful invitation, is almost over.

Let's consider now some of these amazing signs we see now, today:

Huge Highway Engineering, Enormous Cruise Ships, Satellites, Massive Aircraft, Amazing Cities and Skyscrapers, and an Enormous Array of Weapons to kill and destroy including Nuclear Bombs which ended World War 2.

Then we have the most amazing Communication Devices, such as Mobile Phones, Computers, Ipads, Television, and even Artificial Intelligence systems. The whole world, adults, and even children, depend on these devices so much, for records, commerce, banking, travel information, any questions answered instantly, with weird and wonderful games of all descriptions.

Hmmm! Amazing **"increase of knowledge"**, and **"men running to and fro"**!

God has shown us in His Word that all this would happen in the **end times**, so that we can recognise that we are indeed in the time of the feet of iron and clay as in Daniel's image of Chapter 2. From Chapter 7-12, He emphasizes what signs we will see, to know when this sad old world is about to close, when the time of His wonderful loving offer of salvation and eternal life in an earth made new, is about to close.

All this incredible *"increase of knowledge"*, and *"men running to and fro"* <u>has happened just in my short lifetime of nearly 90 years!</u> (As I write this it is 2024. I was born 1935!)

Very soon, probation will be finished! The "**filthy will remain filthy**," and the "**righteous will remain so**", and will be saved from eternal destruction.   Revelation 22:11

Revelation 22 is the very last chapter of God's **LOVE LETTER** to mankind, the **BIBLE**. *Please take a few minutes to read the whole chapter of our Heavenly Father's "summing up" of this whole LOVE story!*

What amazing love of God, to try to alert mankind that **there is a cliff just ahead**, and the end of His wonderful offer of Salvation. Because **He is LOVE**, He cannot allow all this sin and suffering and death, to continue! For this demonstration of His **LOVE**, as opposed to the **FORCE** used by the enemy of God, He has allotted just **six thousand years**. The time He has allowed for this demonstration is about to end, and His people who have learned to know Him and His **LOVE** for His vast creation, will enjoy a Sabbath rest of **one thousand years**, (Revelation 20:5), after which He returns to clean up the mess, and create an eternal home for His people to enjoy and dwell with Him **FOREVER.**

It really is all about LOVE!

CHAPTER 14

TRUST AND OBEY AND LIVE

This chapter shows the amazing advances, and **"increase of knowledge"**, in the field of medicine, from my own personal experience!

It also demonstrates the amazing healing power of the human body, when we follow God's natural laws for living a healthy and happy life.

Monday, 21st March,1988 began as a beautiful morning, and after a good breakfast, and family worship, at about 8.30 am, Graham, my son-in-law, and I decided we'd try to finish clearing the last remaining section of the rear boundary in readiness for fencing the back of our fifty-three-acre property. We only had about eighty or ninety metres to go, and I explained to Graham how to fell the trees within a pre-determined area, by cutting a scarf on one side and then making a cut on the other side a little above the scarf and so on.

The bloodwood tree we chose to cut next was about twenty centimetres in diameter, on the top of a creek bank, and I thought I had explained carefully how and where to drop it. I moved to the bottom of the creek to keep out of his way. After what seemed an unusually long time to put in the first cut, I climbed back up to the top of the creek bank to see what he was doing. He had misunderstood me completely and had cut almost right through the tree at a slight angle.

Just as I approached, the tree moved slightly, and he instinctively ripped the saw backwards at full revs, to avoid jamming it and hit me a terrible blow in the lower right chest.

The revving chain instantly severed at least two ribs and severely lacerated the liver and diaphragm. Blood gushed forth profusely. I quickly gathered the mess of bone, flesh and clothing in my arms and pressed it all together to staunch the bleeding. I then set off to cross the creek and stagger the two to three hundred metres to a vehicle track.

Every breath was sheer agony, but I kept going. Graham, almost beside himself with shock and horror at what had happened, finally caught up with me and knelt in front of me so I could climb on to his broad shoulders. The bumping at each step and trying to control my breathing was unbearable, and I had to ask him to put me down. I sent him off home to get the car and to tell my wife and daughter, Caroline, to bring some towels which I clamped over the gaping wound in my chest to staunch the bleeding.

By then Graham had the car there, and I managed to get myself into the back seat. "Go for it Graham! Caroline and Ruth, (my wife), and the two girls, (my granddaughters), can follow in the other car."

That fifty-kilometre ride to town over poor gravel roads and then bumpy bitumen, was horrific. I had to slow him down, as each bump, as well as trying to breathe, was agony. At the Yandaran cross-roads, I had an overwhelming thirst come over me, and asked Graham to stop and get me a drink out of a container we kept in the boot. The car was an older model Volvo Sports, and as was its habit when hot, the engine snuffed and wouldn't re-start. I had to explain to Graham how to start the motor by shorting out the solenoid points with a screwdriver.

By this time the girls had caught up, and Caroline held her foot on the throttle while Graham tried to find the points I was describing, to short with the screwdriver. Eventually, he found the spot and we were off again at high speed. My wife had climbed in beside me to try to offer comfort and help, as I groaned with the intense pain of each breath, and, as she said later, she wanted to be with me if I didn't make it.

On arrival at Casualty Entrance, I was still very conscious, and able to get out of the car myself. I walked in and a nurse directed me to a wheelchair. A neighbour, Jack Hanks, was there having some sort of treatment, and I acknowledged him and said, "I've got myself cut up with a chainsaw, mate!"

Then it was needles, X-rays and the inevitable questions before I was rushed to an emergency operating theatre, where Doctor McGregor and his team did their very best to sort out the mess. The liver gash was cleaned and packed with some special spray foam. The diaphragm muscle was repaired and sutured. The ribs were repositioned and then wrapped and sewn over with the muscular tissue lining of the chest cavity, to avoid the sharp ends irritating or puncturing the lung. A liver drain was inserted, and then I was hooked up via tubing through my mouth and nose, to a breathing machine, on which my life depended for the next two and a half days in the Intensive Care Unit.

Of course, I knew nothing of all this, as I was completely sedated and immobilized. My loved ones, who took round the clock vigils throughout the whole ordeal, told me all about it after I woke on Thursday morning and began breathing on my own again.

My wife and I are not members of any religious organization or church group, but we are totally committed to our Lord and Saviour Jesus Christ, and we try to live by His moral laws, the **Ten Commandments,** as well as His **Eight Natural Laws of Health.** A simple mnemonic helps me to remember what these eight laws are: **"NEWSTART"**.

Nutrition, **E**xercise, **W**ater, **S**unshine, **T**emperance, **A**ir, **R**est, and **T**rust in God.

For many years, we have followed a Vegan Diet, which means we do not use foods of animal origin. The basic diet recipe is very simple. It is:

"Fruits, Nuts, Grains and Vegetables, prepared in as simple a manner as possible, free from grease."

We live in the fresh air and sunshine of the country. We never use town water unless it is properly filtered. We get plenty of exercise as useful work and refreshing rest. None of the social drugs such as Tea, Coffee, Coke, Alcohol, Tobacco or other Drugs are ever used in our home, and we try to be temperate in our use of even the good things. Most of all, we trust in our Omniscient Creator and His promises, that if we will obey His wonderful laws, given solely for our benefit to protect and guide us, He will indeed bless and care for His people.

Accordingly, my wife asked me on Thursday morning, if I'd like to be anointed as per instructions for the sick as given in James chapter Five of the Holy Scriptures. At that stage, I could not see through the **"valley of the shadow"**, and I asked her to arrange it for me. She quickly rang some Christian friends, Dean Armytage and his dad, who live near Boonah south of Brisbane, and they agreed to journey up to Bundaberg as soon as possible to comply with my request.

My father rang the hospital from Bowen on Tuesday, and later on when he visited me on Sunday, he told me how he'd contacted the Sister in ICU by phone. She had told him that I was very seriously hurt, but that my blood had tested out as nigh on perfect, which, she said, was a very big plus in my favour. I had specifically requested not to be given blood, as I did not want to risk the wogs that are sometimes transmitted in this way today. If blood was needed at all, my son-in-law, Graham, had offered to give of his, as he has the same blood type. Even though I had lost a great deal of blood, I did not need a transfusion and had full colour again in a few days. **What a marvelous machine is the human body!**

My daughter, Jennelle, arrived from Sydney on Thursday, and joined Caroline and Wendy, (my second daughter), and my wife Ruth, in the long vigils. Even though heavily sedated and totally immobilized for those two and a half days on the Life Support Machines, their voices and touches registered with me. This was clearly indicated by the instant variations in beeps and wave patterns as recorded by the heart monitoring device. They noticed this very interesting phenomenon each time they spoke to me or touched me. It was so encouraging to have my loved ones nearby. It gave me the courage to hang on, and strengthened my determination to live, even though I was not conscious!

On Friday morning, I was supposed to go back into theatre, for further sorting out and exploration under general anaesthetic. When Doctor McGregor removed the dressings and examined the wound early on Friday morning, he just stood there looking intently at it, and never said a word for fully a minute or two. What was he looking at? Why didn't he say something? Was the wound fly-blown? Was he wondering how to tell me I'd need a liver transplant? All sorts of morbid thoughts ran through my mind. After what seemed an age, he looked incredulously at me and said, "This wound wants to heal itself! I won't need to use general anaesthetic. I can tidy it all up, remove the drainpipe, and put in a few more stitches under local anaesthetic this morning!" What a relief! **Again, what a wonderful body machine! What incredible healing mechanisms God has put within this masterpiece of all His vast creation!**

I was still apprehensive about it all and wondering if it would be possible that Dean and his Dad would arrive in time, to do the anointing service before the return to theatre, scheduled for later that morning. Late morning, mid-day, early afternoon all came and went, and about 3pm Dean and his father arrived. We asked the nurse for permission to draw the curtain and proceeded with the anointing ceremony as outlined in the Scriptures in James 5. Almost as soon as we had finished, the nurse came and advised that theatre was ready for me. I went off assured that my Maker was with me, and the Master Physician was in charge of my case.

As the final work was to be done under local anaesthetic, I was able to watch the whole thing in the overhead mirrors and assist as required. Doctor McGregor was temporarily called away to an adjoining theatre, so a younger surgeon offered to do the job, and asked if I'd like him to tidy it up a bit to which I agreed. He straightened the ragged edges of the wound with his scalpel, and then carefully and neatly sutured it all together. Then the large plastic drainpipe had to come out of the chest, where it had been inserted in its own special hole, to drain the lung area, after the lower lobe of the lung had collapsed earlier on from fluid build-up. The flesh had grown so tightly around it, and it took quite a deal of pulling to remove it, while I held my breath to prevent air entering the chest cavity before the hole was tightly closed with a 'purse-string' suture technique. Just as young Doctor Cliff completed the job, Doctor McGregor arrived and remarked at what a "pretty job" they had done of it.

From the start, fluids, food, and some medications were administered via a drip into my arm, and all fluids from my bladder were measured carefully via another line and catheter from the urinary tract, and records kept on my charts.

On Saturday morning, I was surprised to find myself experiencing a very definite urge to use my bowels. Eventually, I had to call for a second pan. My bowels worked perfectly, passing the remains of breakfast the previous Monday of the accident. As the doctor explained, at the time of the accident, the stomach went into severe shock and ceased all activity allowing the body to direct all its energies to the healing process, till the crisis was over. **Again, what an amazing, remarkable organism!**

Saturday morning also brought a light fluid diet, which I was ready for, and even longing for something more substantial. My bowels worked perfectly from then on.

Very early on Sunday morning, the drip entry to my arm began to be very painful. I eventually had to call the sister in charge, who immediately removed it and called the night doctor. He verified that the vein had broken down and was leaking fluid into the surrounding tissues. After checking the charts, he advised that the drip could be discontinued, as all outgoing fluids were perfectly clear and of the correct amounts. I was loosed from the other undignified tie to my bladder on Sunday morning and I was free again at last!

What a thrill to be able to stand upright and walk about again, to wash myself, and visit about the wards to share experiences and encourage the other poor suffering people there. What a miracle to have had such a serious injury, and yet be up and about only days after the accident occurred! I stand amazed myself at the incredible speed of recovery the human body is capable of, when that body is properly managed and cared for according to the **"Manufacturer's Manual"**.

Also on Sunday morning, the local newspaper reporter and photographer who'd heard about the accident and miraculous recovery, arrived, and as a result, the Bundaberg Newsmail carried a large front-page picture and write-up about the whole thing, in the Wednesday, 30th March issue. (See Appendix A)

About a week later, on Thursday, April 7th, Newsmail printed my letter to the Editor, in which I expressed sincere thanks to all who'd helped me through my traumatic experience. (See Appendix B)

On Sunday evening, after the last of a long line of visitors had left, I went off to the shower and enjoyed my first decent bath since admission. The hot water flowing over the wound area felt so soothing, that I found myself reluctant to turn off the hot water tap, to finish with my usual full cold rinse off. I felt so refreshed after the shower, that I asked the sister in charge if I might wander downstairs to the ICU to thank the Staff there for their care. She rang through to make sure they were not busy, and I was able to visit and chat with them for some time, finding out what they had done to me, (See Medical Superintendent's Report Appendix C), and sharing with them my lifestyle, which undoubtedly was largely responsible for my swift recovery. I arrived back in the ward about 10pm and was able to catch a few winks of sleep. Casualty wards are not conducive to sleep, especially when one is used to the peace and quiet of the Australian bush.

Monday morning brought Doctor McGregor to check me out, and I was greeted with,

"Well, how's this fellow with the liver that heals itself?"

"He's ready for home!" was the patient's reply.

"Now hold on there. Not so fast. I'll need some liver function tests, and perhaps tomorrow....."

He ordered a complete liver function test and other blood tests and changed the diet to light solids.

By now, the light diet was really being relished, and was supplemented with lovely fresh fruit, nuts and lots of dark organic grape juice supplied by my family. The poor dietician was quite non-plussed to know what to feed me, so I sent her the simple recipe, as quoted earlier, and things improved considerably.

Tuesday morning, 29th March, eventually came around and the doctor arrived. Could I go home today? Yes! All liver function tests were perfectly normal. He advised me to be very careful, and not to attempt anything that might undo the knitting process, and to come and see him in a few weeks' time.

So, on Tuesday morning, 29th March, after visiting around the ward and giving each person a little Gospel gift booklet, and thanking the Staff for their care, I walked out of the hospital, not completely fit yet, but well enough to go home, to enjoy sun-baths, herbal teas and poultices, bushwalks, and best of all, uninterrupted rest in my own bed, with my beloved wife and companion to care for me. And this **JUST EIGHT DAYS** after a terrible injury which could easily have ended my life. I just praise my Maker continually for, as King David said in Psalms 139:14, **"I am fearfully and wonderfully made. Marvellous are Thy works, and that my soul knoweth right well."**

Isn't our Creator an amazing LOVING Father?

CHAPTER 15

THIS SEQUEL IS ALSO AMAZING

A few weeks later, I returned to have Doctor McGregor do a check-up. He sent me for an X-ray, and when viewing it he just stood gazing at it for quite some time without saying a word. Then he turned to me and very deliberately said with great conviction,

"Don, if you had not been living as you have for some time, you would most likely not be alive today. And what's more... if I had not seen what happened to you with my own eyes, I would not believe what has happened to you as this X-ray looks like a perfectly normal chest!"

I could not help exclaiming, "Praise the Lord!"

My sincere thanks go out to the whole medical and ancillary Staff of the Bundaberg Base Hospital. I found them to be really skilled, caring wonderful people. My sincere thanks also to all who helped and encouraged me and prayed for me in my hour of need.

Most of all my thanks must go to my Maker and my Redeemer, Who saw fit to answer the many prayers offered, and Who helped me in such a remarkable and miraculous way.

My hope and prayer now is that this experience and my testimony here, may perhaps be the means of encouraging others to follow the laws our Maker has given us to run this wonderful human machinery, for long lasting, smooth and trouble-free operation. Should you happen to accidentally damage this body machine as I did, may you also see the incredible self-healing powers latent within the human body, properly run and maintained in harmony with the unchangeable laws of our Creator.

Thank you for reading my testimony, and now more than fourteen years later, there is **ANOTHER SEQUEL** that has to be told! It is another wonderful example of how God can use us for His plan, to save others, if we are fully committed to Him!

It is another example of God's LOVE, even implanted in His creatures!

CHAPTER 16

ANOTHER AMAZING OUTCOME

When one commits his life wholly to God and His service, I believe that accidents which happen always have a reason, and I really believe that true committed Christians do not have 'accidents'.... they have 'incidents'. In Romans 8: 28, the Apostle Paul says,

"All things work together for good to them that love God; to them who are called according to His purpose." Well, how could my experience possibly work for good?

I have had my testimony written up in the New Idea (See Appendix D) and broadcast over Radio and TV. Literally millions of people have read my story. I have been able through my testimony, to help dozens of people to understand the laws of their being and have seen these folks change their lifestyle and return to good health and strength by following God's laws. This is a continual ongoing opportunity to show everyone with whom I am acquainted, a healthier lifestyle here, and also to help 'whosoever will', to take hold on eternal life.

But the most thrilling outcome, happened about three years ago now, in 1997, while I was in Townsville shopping in "Woollies" one Friday afternoon. My mobile rang, and a man's voice identified himself as Barry Mason from Charters Towers. I did not remember a Barry Mason. He went on to say:

"Don, I was in hospital with you in Bundaberg, and before you left you gave me a 'little Gospel book' and I've been trying to track you down for some time, because I want you to teach me how to be a Christian!"

Next day was the Creator's special day -- the Sabbath, so I suggested that Barry come to Townsville, and we'd have a real Bible Study time together as he was only an hour away. We had over three hours of wonderful fellowship and study of God's Word.

As I had to return to our home in Kingaroy, I introduced Barry to some wonderful Christian friends, Les and Del Morgan, who live up on Harvey's Range west of Townsville, and they helped Barry to fully understand the major truths of God's Word and fellowshipped with him often. Then I had a phone call about two years ago now...

"Don, I want you to come up to Townsville and baptize me!"

Of course, I was overjoyed to do this for him. We travelled again to Townsville and baptized Barry into Christ and His church, in Les and Del's pool. Barry is still growing and happy in the Lord and is leading his family in His footsteps also. Praise to our Wonderful God!

If anyone reading this testimony, would like a FREE copy of a 'little Gospel booklet', just let me have your name and address and it will be on its way! For real meaning and purpose in life, just....

TRUST AND OBEY AND LIVE!

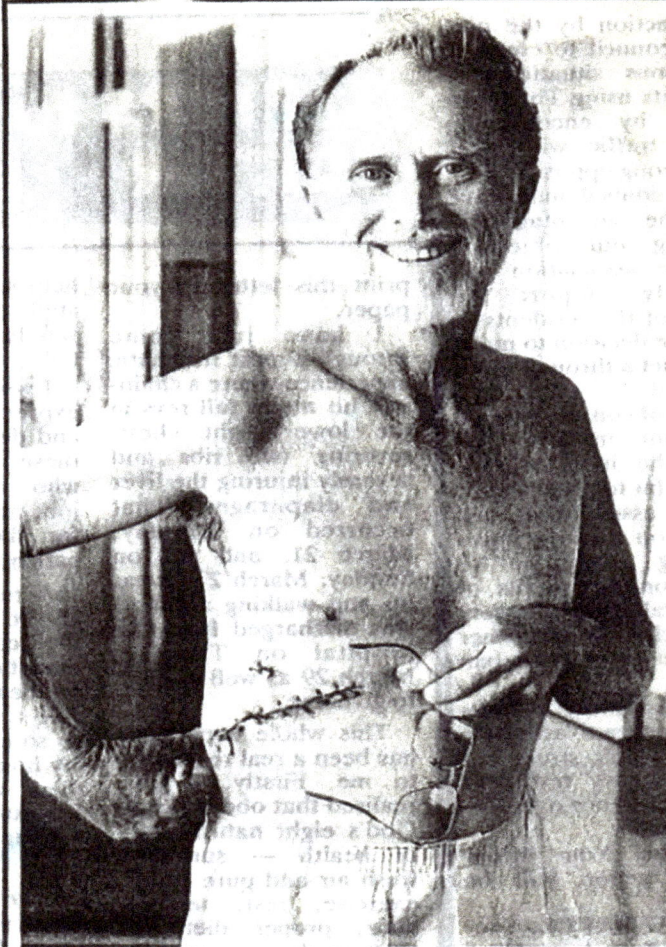

● Mr Don Menkins displays the scar left by a chainsaw. "I thought I'd had it."

Miracle, says man who survives chainsaw accident

A man who survived a deep gash from a chainsaw last week said he believes in miracles.

Mr Don Menkins, aged 52, said there was no other explanation for his "incredible recovery" than his belief in the Bible and in clean, healthy living.

Mr Menkins was injured when cutting trees on his property at Yandaran last week. His son-in-law, Mr Graham Baird, was slicing through a tree when the chainsaw dragged suddenly free.

It struck Mr Menkins across his right side, severing two ribs, chopping out a piece of his liver and badly injuring his diaphragm.

Mr Menkins described the pain as excruciating. He clasped his arms around the wound, which bled profusely, and staggered to the road to get in the car.

"I thought I'd had it . . . blood gushed everywhere," Mr Menkins said. "I grabbed everything tight and pressed . . . trying to breathe with a cut-up diaphragm," he said.

"It is a miracle of God and the tremendous healing power in my body."

Mr Menkins was released from Bundaberg Base Hospital yesterday.

(Appendix A)

haste action by the previous council to create a dangerous situation for residents using Thabeban Street by encouraging heavy traffic will meet with strong opposition.

The council may have had the advantage by ignoring our objection but the association will certainly support the wishes of the residents to have the decision to make this street a through road, modified.

Lack of consultation on important matters that affect the lives of residents is far too prevalent.

The association will prevail on the new town planning committee to confer on the merits of heavy traffic versus safety for the children and other regular users of Thabeban Street.

It took almost 20 years of persistence to acquire a result for this street but not for heavy traffic to have precedence over local dwellers.

No Sirs. Your inconsiderate action will be opposed.

**E. G. BAUER,
President, Avenell
Heights Progress
Association, Ashfield
Road.**

● Thanks!

When one's heart is just so full and bubbling over with gratitude to God and to one's fellow man, how can I be silent and fall back into an everyday pattern of living.

I want to tell the world and so I would be grateful if you could find space to

LETTERS to the EDITOR

print this letter in your paper.

I have just come through a most traumatic experience where a chainsaw hit me at full revs in the lower right chest, severing two ribs and severely injuring the liver and diaphragm. That occurred on Monday, March 21, and yet on Sunday, March 27, I was up and walking about. I was discharged from the hospital on Tuesday, March 29 as well enough to go home.

This whole experience has been a real revelation to me. Firstly, I have realised that obedience to God's eight natural laws of health — sunshine, fresh air and pure water, exercise, rest, temperance, proper diet and trust in divine power — brings increasing resistance to disease and a much happier, healthier body with tremendous healing power within the human organism to heal itself.

Secondly, I would like the people of this city and the readers of this newspaper to know that we have a facility — the Bundaberg Base Hospital — with skilled professional and anciliary staff second to none. Without the skilled professional

help so quickly and ably applied to myself, I would simply be another statistic!

I would like to publicly express my sincere thanks and deep gratitude to all these wonderful people who really know their job, and who really care for the needs of each patient local or otherwise.

A really big thank you also to the Red Cross for the convenient accommodation provided for my dear ones, who were able to stay in town and be so close by my side in my hour of need. Having them so close gave me assurance and inspiration to hang on.

My sincere gratitude also to two brethren of God's remnant people. — Dean Armytage and his dad — who drove all the way from Boonah to answer my call for anointing as in James 5.

Most of all, however, my deepest thanks must go to God who saw fit to answer these prayers and heal me in such a miraculous way. I am not a member of any denomination, but I love my Saviour dearly and my life and all I possess is totally dedicated to Him in every respect.

**D. MENKENS,
Tekoa,
Greenlea Road,
Yandaran.**

(Appendix B)

BUNDABERG *Hospitals Board*

BUNDABERG. Q. 4670.

All Communications to be
addressed to The Manager

In reply please quote
this Number

ps/lm

27th. April, 1988.

TO WHOM IT MAY CONCERN.

Mr. Donald Menkens was admitted to Bundaberg Base Hospital on 21/3/88 after a chain saw accident when he was hit on the right side of his chest.

This resulted in a large laceration and he was taken to theatre that night where he had a deep laceration to his liver. This was stitched and packed. A large laceration of his right diaphragm was also sutured.

Post operatively he was ventilated and suffered a collapse of the base of his right lung. Extubation was performed on the 23/3/88 and from that time onwards he made good progress. The remaining wound was closed on the 25/3/88 and he was subsequently discharged on the 29/3/88.

This indeed was a serious laceration to the upper abdomen resulting in considerable blood loss with damage to the lung, diaphragm and liver.

P. SWEENEY.
MEDICAL SUPERINTENDENT.

(Appendix C)

Don Menkens: a chainsaw couldn't sever his faith

Happy and healthy, this teacher turned farmer attributes his amazing recovery to his religious beliefs

Don Menkens can still vividly recall the second his son-in-law pulled back a high-revving chainsaw, and the shock as the teeth tore into his side just above the waist.

Out in the bush and 50km from the nearest hospital, the accident would have killed most men. But Don, 52, a devoutly religious man, was back at work on his property eight days later.

Don, his wife Ruth, one of their daughters Caroline and her husband Graham, were living on a property north of Bundaberg, Queensland. Don and Graham had been clearing trees for fencing on the property when the accident happened.

After showing Graham, a manual arts teacher, how to fell a tree with a chainsaw (by making a cut on one side and then a wedge on the other to control the angle of fall), Don was working in a creek bed with a crowbar and an axe.

He was waiting for Graham to fell the tree, but when nothing happened he climbed up from the creek and approached Graham from behind.

"As I got near him I could see he hadn't made the other cut, but was trying to go straight through the tree in one go," Don says. "Just as I got to him, the tree lurched and Graham panicked, thinking he was going to jam the saw. He ripped the chainsaw back.

● **Don Menkens at the scene of his accident.**

"I saw it coming and this was the vision I was to have for some time afterwards. It was revving flat out and as I jumped back to avoid it I put my arm up to protect myself."

Fortunately, as it turned out, the spinning teeth missed Don's arm and tore into the right side of his chest. In an instant two ribs were severed, the diaphragm slashed and his liver lacerated.

"It just happened so quickly; it was instantaneous," Don recalls.

Graham, according to Don, stood riveted to the spot, the chainsaw still in his hand, already going into shock. Don immediately went into a crouch and, with his hands covered in dirt and grime from his labors, started shoving back the parts of him that emerged from the gaping wound.

"I was trying to pick up the mess, shove it back in and stop the blood flow. I knew I had to stop it somehow."

By the time Graham had snapped back to reality, Don was already 30m through the bush

(Appendix D)

● Don and wife Ruth . . . they made a 50km mercy dash to hospital.

heading for his wife and daughter in their cabin 100m away.

"The pain was indescribable, I knew I had to get moving." Don says. "I was trying to breathe but the saw had cut through the diaphragm. Every breath was agony because all the muscles around it had been mangled.

"I was still dragging myself along when Graham started screaming, 'Dad, Dad, wait, I'll carry you'.

"I knew if I tried to get on his back it would be impossible to hold everything in. But eventually he raced up in front of me — and he's a big lad — knelt down and told me to get on. So I got on his back and there was blood and gore all over him — it was even in his hair.

"But as he strode along through the bush the pain was just unbearable. I had to get him to put me down and go the rest of the way on his own. I just couldn't bear it."

While Don squatted by a bush track, Graham sprinted to the cabin and Caroline and Ruth rushed back with a towel to staunch the blood. Graham came down in Don's car and put him in the back seat. Ruth and Caroline took another car.

"Graham took off fast but I had to get him to slow down. Every bump was agony," Don says.

They had 50 tortuous kilometres ahead of them over dirt roads and bumpy bitumen to get to Bundaberg Base Hospital, but 20km into the journey Don had to get Graham to stop to get him a drink of water from a container in the boot.

While Don was slaking his parched throat the car's engine sputtered and died, as it had done before.

"I had to instruct Graham to short the points with a screwdriver," Don recalls. "By that time Caroline and Ruth had turned up and Caroline held the accelerator down while Graham eventually found the right points."

Although every second counted, with Don losing blood at an alarming rate, the family didn't panic.

"I was surprised Don stayed conscious all the way to the hospital. He didn't want me to touch him. He knew what he was doing," Ruth says.

When they finally arrived at the hospital, Don walked unaided into the casualty section.

"I must have been really and truly conscious," Don says. "I saw my neighbor in casualty when I walked in. I waved to him and explained that I'd just had a bit of an accident with a chainsaw.

"He got really mad with the doctors because they were fussing over him. I remember him saying, 'Leave me alone. That man is my neighbor and he's dying.'"

Doctors were amazed at the speed of Don's recovery.

A former teacher and now a farmer spreading the word of the Seventh Day Adventist Church near Boonah in south-eastern Queensland, Don lives according to the teachings of the church.

"It's a simple philosophy," he says, explaining his good health. "There are laws of health: sunshine; fresh air; pure water; proper rest; exercise; temperance, which includes leaving alone alcohol, tobacco, tea and coffee; a pure diet of fruits, grains, nuts and vegetables; moderation in all things; and faith in the divine power."

Don's faith, now unshakeable, has spread to his children and 10 grandchildren, who, he says, were never as convinced as he was.

"It has cemented in my own mind that this is the way to live and it has turned my family's thinking around too. They are starting to believe there is truth in what I have been telling them.

"If, in the long run, it enables them to be healthy and happy, then that's all a father can want for his children.

"I continue to be amazed at the incredible powers of the body. It is true, we are fearfully and wonderfully made."

Story: Graham Bicknell
Pictures: Doug Drummond

NEW IDEA, 28/1/89 13

Well, my wife and I have had many other wonderful experiences where we have seen the Hand of our loving God working miracle after miracle in our lives, as we have worked for Him at home and abroad, as missionary teachers and natural therapists for more than sixty years.

In Paul's book to the Romans chapter 8 and verse 28, he reminds us all again, that,

"All things work together for good to them that love God and are called according to His purpose". Romans 8:28

Please take note… It's all about LOVE.

CHAPTER 17

CHOOSING---THE GIFT OF LOVE

Since the time of Adam and Eve, men have been rejecting the Creator. After they sinned by believing the Serpent's lies, that they wouldn't die, but would become wise and become like God. God still loved them and gave them a wonderful promise. It is found in Genesis 3:15.

"God, (speaking to Satan) **said, "I will put enmity,** (open hostility), **between thee and the woman, and between thy seed and her seed,** (children, offspring). **He,** (Jesus), **shall bruise thy head, and thou** (Satan) **shalt bruise His heel."**

Where would a wound hurt you fatally? Certainly not my heel, but my head! In clear language, the Serpent, Satan, Lucifer, and his followers, would be fatally wounded and die!

God had promised Adam and Eve that there would be a Deliverer, a Saviour, who would give "the seed of the woman", (all mankind), the opportunity to **choose** to accept Jesus as Lord and Saviour, and the amazing free gift of salvation, with eternal life in an earth made new. What love from a loving God!

It's all about love!

But, you probably know the story!

Cain was eventually born and Eve said, **"I have gotten a man from the Lord!"** Genesis 4:1.

She thought it was the promised Deliverer! Abel was also their second child to be born.

God had asked Adam and Eve and their two children to bring an innocent little lamb and kill it, offering it as a sacrifice, which would remind them of His promise to send a Saviour.

Cain disobeyed, **chose** to do his own will, and brought an offering of fruits and other produce. Cain's offering was not accepted by the Lord, because it was not what He had asked them to do!

He had told them to bring an inocent little lamb to be killed and offered as a sacrifice, which would remind them of the coming Redeemer Who would be killed, to make atonement for sin!

Cain was very angry and **chose** to kill his brother Abel! What a shocking example of what is happening today, as those who **choose** to be Satan's seed, are commiting heinous crimes and killing someone nearly every day in the news, completely opposite to what God has written in His unchanging law and His laws of **LOVE!**

Why did men decide to build the **Tower of Babel?** They did not want to accept God and wanted their own way, to do as they pleased! They became so wicked that God changed their language into the many different languages we see today. This confused them greatly and so the different groups speaking similarly, moved off to different areas of the earth!

There were many more examples of how men tried to get rid of God, till the time of Noah, for example. Noah tried to warn the people for a hundred and twenty years, while He did what God told him to do in building a huge boat. Anyone who **chose** to accept God's warnings could enter the Ark and be saved from the worldwide flood. Even when the people saw the animals coming and entering this huge ship, they still **chose** to reject God's offer of salvation. Only eight faithful souls entered the Ark and were saved! You can read all about it in the Bible in Genesis Chapters 6 to 11.

Then there is the example of Sodom and Gommorah and three other very evil cities. Again men had become so wicked rejecting God's law and doing their own will, that God destroyed those cities as I have written about earlier. Only Lot and his two daughters **chose** to do as they were told and left the cities before God sent fiery balls of sulphur upon them. Those sulphur balls are still visible today as I have described earlier. The remains of these cities are still visible today if you care to go and see for yourself!

As time went on, we find Babylon with Nebuchadnezzar as ruler, who thought he could be in charge of the world, even though God warned him in a vivid dream. Daniel was able to tell the King what he had dreamed and what it meant, but what did Nebuchadnezzar do? He **chose** to build a great golden image of himself totally of **Gold,** and ordered all the people at a certain time to bow down and worship it! This was in flagrant violation of the second of God's Ten Commandments.

God's law says not to make an image of anything or bow down to it. You can read the whole account in Exodus 20 and in Daniel chapter 3.

It is interesting to note that there were three Hebrew young men, Shadrach, Meshach and Abednego, who **chose** not to disobey God's express command, and did not bow down as the king had commanded, even though they knew that the king had decreed that anyone who did not bow down would be cast into a blazing fiery furnace. God miraculously saved those three faithful boys who determined to obey God come what may! You can read all about this amazing story in Exodus 20 and Daniel 3! It really shows God's amazing love for his faithful people.

It's all about love!

I personally want to stand true to my loving Heavenly Father no matter what I may have to face. As dear Job says in his book, after all the trials he suffered at the hands of the enemy of God; **"Though He slay me, yet will I trust Him!"** Job 13:15-18.

One of my favourite quotes, from an inspired author always challenges me. It says;

"The greatest want of the world, is the want of men!

-Men who will not be bought or sold!

-Men who in their inmost souls are true and honest!

-Men who do not fear to call sin by it's right name!

-Men whose conscience is as true to duty as the needle to the pole!

-Men who will stand for the right though the heavens fall!"

The **six days, ("a day with the Lord is as a thousand years")**, (2 Peter 3:8), will be followed by a **Sabbath rest of one thousand years**, (as one day with the Lord). The people of God, the raised ones, and the living at the time of His coming, will enjoy that thousand-year Sabbath of rest with God in heaven. I Thessalonians 4: 13-18.

During this time, the Devil will be chained and unable to do his dastardly work! Check with the infallible Word of God, in Revelation 20: 1-3 and onwards. See Jeremiah 4: 23-25. It's all there in the Word of God!

God has allotted a specific time for this demonstration before His Universe. The Bible translators have said <u>Jesus</u> doesn't even know when the end will be. The same original word can also mean, "makes known". Jesus, is the **Word**, and is also **God**, (John 1:1), so of course He will know when the time of probation is to end but, **His Father is the One Who will make the announcement!**

When He says "Enough", the time of probation will end, just as in the time of Noah. Just as the door of the Ark was shut on that great ship, then it will be too late to accept His offer of eternal life with Him, in an earth He has promised to make over, brand new as it was at first, when He completed Creating the Earth and everything in it.

We will be able to enjoy only joy and happiness, and there will never be any sin, suffering or death forever! Our God is offering an "endless hope" for all mankind, instead of a "hopeless end!" He still will give each one of His people, including the angels, and any other beings He's created, **FREE WILL!**

But.... because He has for six thousand years, allowed the demonstration of His Kingdom of **LOVE**, in total conflict with the kingdom of Satan, who rules by **FORCE**, all of His vast Creation will have witnessed His love, the crowning act of which was when He offered His only begotten Son, as an atonement for sin. John 3:16 & 17.

Consider carefully how the Universe and all its inhabitants, from the greatest being, to the minutest atom, will immediately thank our loving God Who will be perfectly justified in removing anything or anyone who <u>chooses </u>to try to bring in selfishness and FORCE, which is the opposite of LOVE.

<u>*His creation will retain FREEWILL forever, but the demonstration is over and will never need*</u> <u>*to be repeated!*</u> *All His vast Creation will know why He protects all who love Him! As an eternal reminder, our blessed Saviour will forever bear the marks of His crucifixion.*

Please forgive me for repeating myself so much, but, God really loves His unique creation **and His special beings He created in His own image.**

It truly is all about LOVE!

CHAPTER 18

BIRTH & EARLY LIFE OF JESUS

Have you ever stopped long enough to contemplate the realities of the birth of Jesus?

At the very beginning of God's Word, the Bible, in Genesis 1:1, it says, **"In the beginning <u>GOD</u> created the heavens and the earth."**

In the Gospel of John 1:1 and 2, it starts off with exactly the same Truth;

"In the beginning was the Word, and the Word was with God, and <u>the Word was God</u>." <u>THAT "WORD" WAS GOD THE ETERNAL CREATOR!</u>

In verse 3 it says, **"All things were made by Him; and without Him was not anything made that was made."**

Then in verse 14 it says, **"<u>And the Word was made flesh</u>, and dwelt among us, and we beheld His glory, the glory as of the only begotten of the Father, full of grace and truth."**

Let's look at what God did closely and remember that this tiny baby that was to be born and become flesh, was the only begotten Son of our Heavenly Father. **He was really the Omnipotent, Omniscient, Omnipresent, Eternal God, the Creator!** He experienced the very same entry into this world as every human being does, just as you and I did, but in a very different and difficult situation.

He was born of a virgin. He was carried in His mother's womb for nine months. **Remember, this is the Creator of the universe!**

According to Jewish Law, a woman found to be pregnant before marriage would be accused of adultery and would be punished or put away!

Joseph, who was betrothed to Mary, knew he had not been with her, and was not responsible for this pregnancy. He still loved her dearly, and **"was not mindful to put her away"**. Matthew 1:19

While he was wondering what to do, the angel Gabriel came to him with a message from God the Father. He told Joseph not to be afraid to take Mary as his wife, as the child she was carrying and was developing in her womb, was conceived by the Holy Ghost. This child would be the One, as promised to Adam and Eve, over four thousand years ago, after they disobeyed God's explicit instructions, and believed the Serpent, Lucifer! (See Genesis chapter 2 and 3).

God still loved them dearly and promised them a Redeemer would come, to bear the results of sin, and provide salvation for whoever would **choose** to accept His loving and amazing offer of Redemption. You can read all about it in Luke's Gospel, Chapter 2 and onwards.

While Mary was heavy with child, a command went forth from the Roman Emperor, Caesar Augustus, requiring everyone to return to their hometown for registration and taxation purposes.

So, Joseph and Mary had to travel to the city of David, Bethlehem, because they were of the house and lineage of David.

There were no cars, buses, trains, aeroplanes, or ships to travel in, and they didn't even have horse and cart! So, they left Nazareth, to travel back to Bethlehem. As Mary was nearing birth time, Joseph put her on a donkey, with very little luggage, food or water for the journey. When they eventually arrived there, every hotel, and motel had "No Vacancy" signs up.

Now I've never been pregnant, but most of you mothers reading this would know what it must have been like for dear Mary. Perhaps her "water had broken", already! There were no ambulances, hospitals, doctors or nurses nearby. Just dear Joseph and Mary! What were they to do?

Finally, Joseph found an old cattle-shed, and carried Mary inside and laid her down on the floor on some old straw. Perhaps there were animals there as well, wondering what was happening, and noisily voicing their surprise at such unexpected visitors! It certainly was not a hygienic place to have a baby!

Remember, this is where the **Great I AM, the WORD, the CREATOR of the Universe**, was to be born as the "the only begotten of the Father"! How incredible, and what an amazing demonstration of His love for His Creation. All the heavenly angels and whatever other beings God had created throughout His Universe, were all watching this demonstration of the love of God! Yes, we sing, "Away in a manger, no crib for a bed," but have you ever stopped to think about the realities of it all?

Now Mary is really suffering birth pains and only Joseph was there to comfort and encourage her. Eventually, the baby was born, and Joseph no doubt, had to do the separating of mother and baby by cutting the umbilical cord. No doubt, the little One began to cry as babies do. Then Joseph wrapped the little baby boy in whatever cloth he had with him and held Him close. After that, Joseph placed Him on Mary's chest, to find her breasts, to start sucking for milk, like any other baby. Then they laid Him down in a feeding trough to sleep! **This is the Great I AM, the Creator of the Universe!**

What a beautiful painting by a talented artist of the baby Jesus, our Creator, with Mary His mother, and dear Joseph, in a Cattle Shed.

In the beginning was the Word, and the Word was with God and the Word was God! The same was in the beginning with God. All things were made by Him and without Him was not anything made that was made. He was the Creator, the Word, Who became flesh and dwelt amongst us, and we beheld His glory, the glory as of the only begotten of the Father, full of grace and truth. John 1:1-3, 14.

Are you saying I'm being too imaginative? I'm simply trying to picture the realities of all this! How humbling, how lowly God stooped to show us His unfathomable **love**! The whole story is told by Luke. So please find your Bible and read of this amazing story in detail, in Luke's first few chapters.

Yes, it's all about LOVE!

CHAPTER 19

REALITY CONTINUED

Mary and Joseph had to clean up, with no electric lights, water, toilets, showers and few clean clothes. While they were wondering what to do next, they were visited by some shepherds, who saw hosts of angels heralding Jesus' birth, while they were minding their sheep at night in a paddock nearby. Obviously, the angels had told the shepherds where to go, to find this precious baby, Who would be the promised Redeemer. So, they found the old cattle shed and saw the tiny baby, the **CREATOR OF THE UNIVERSE**, with His mother Mary and Joseph.

Also, it seems that while they were still in the shed, three wise men from the east visited, following a moving star which stopped over the cattle shed. They were not even Jewish people, but they brought lots of gold, frankincense and myrrh, as presents for Joseph and Mary, which would help them with expenses for what was coming.

When eight days had passed, Mary and Joseph took baby Jesus to the temple to have His foreskin removed, (called circumcision), as was the custom of the Jewish people. While there, Simeon and Anna both prophets, held the tiny baby and blessed Him as the promised **Redeemer**. You can read about this too, again in Luke's Gospel, chapter 2: 21-39. Remember, this baby is **the Son of God!**

Not long after this they had to flee to Egypt, again by donkey transport, as Herod had sent out a command to have every male baby in the vicinity of Bethlehem, two years old and under to be killed. What terrible anguish and grief experienced for all the parents of this shocking massacre of their children, by the selfish tyrant who didn't want any opposition to his rule. This too, is all recorded in the Gospel of Matthew 2:16-18.

Eventually, they were able to travel back to Nazareth, where Joseph set up a cabinet shop making furniture, with funds provided by the visiting wise men from the east. In this way Joseph was able to provide for their needs. Joseph and Mary taught young Jesus how to read and write in a Home-School situation. No doubt they taught Him from the Scriptures, about the Promised One Who would one day come and be the Redeemer promised to our first parents, Adam and Eve.

Joseph and Mary had other babies who grew up to be brothers and sisters of Jesus. You can read about this in Matthew 13:55 and Mark 6:3.

As Jesus grew up, no doubt He played with other boys and girls of His age, who played all sorts of games as children do. In a Home School situation, Mary and Joseph taught Jesus as a young boy, and through teenage years, other subjects as well. They also taught Him about the Words of God in the only Scriptures then available, the Old Testament!

When Jesus was 12 years old, Joseph and Mary took Him with them to the temple in Jerusalem with a large group of relatives and friends, at Passover time. Luke 2: 41-52.

When the festivities were over and believing that Jesus was with the other young people, they all set off to travel back to their respective homes. At the end of the first day of happy travel together, they all set up their tents and prepared for their evening meals. That's when Joseph and Mary realised that Jesus was not with them. They asked everywhere but could not find him and became anxious. So, they set out to return to Jerusalem to try to find Him.

After three days of searching, they found Him in the temple speaking with the church leaders. When Mary asked why Jesus had not come with them, He said, **"Didn't you know that I must be about My Father's business?"** Luke 2:49

Even at just twelve years of age, Jesus knew why He was here on earth, to do His Father's will, as prophesied in the Word of God in the Old Testament. These were the only Scriptures then available.

Remember, this is the **Great I AM, the Eternal Son of God, the Redeemer,** promised to our first parents after they **chose** to believe the Serpent, Lucifer, instead of obeying their Heavenly Father and His specific command. Before this rejection of God by our first parents, the Father, Son and Holy Spirit had a plan in place, **before the world began,** (Ephesians 1:29), to offer Salvation and eternal life again to Adam and Eve, and all who would come after them, even to the **"time of the end"**, **to the time of you and me.** This amazing plan shows the wonderful love of God, to anyone who will **choose** to accept God's love and keep His Law of **love**!

Again, it's all about LOVE!

CHAPTER 20

HIS MINISTRY BEGINS

Eventually, as a family they arrived back in Nazareth. Joseph continued having Jesus work with him, making cabinets and other furniture to sell to people who needed them, till He was thirty years old. Now it was AD 27 as we say today in our calendars. Jesus no doubt thanked Joseph and Mary for caring for him all those years, and then set off on His special mission for His Father in heaven.

The Scripture narrative says Jesus travelled from Galilee to Jordan, to be baptized by John the Baptist who was teaching people about the coming Messiah. When Jesus asked John to baptise Him, John said, "No! I need to be baptised by You!" Jesus asked John to go ahead and baptise Him to fulfil the Scripture prophecy in Isaiah 7: 10-14.

When He arose from the water after John baptised Him, the Spirit of God descended upon Him like a dove, and a Voice from the heavens was heard saying, **"This is My beloved Son, in Whom I am well pleased."** Luke 3:21,22.

This was AD 27 which is the start of the last week of years, of the 70 weeks of years prophecy, found in chapter 9: 24-27 of the book of Daniel. This is the amazing prophecy I dealt with in Chapter 12 of this book.

Another beautiful painting of John the Baptist baptizing Jesus in the Jordan. Luke 3:21-22

Now as Jesus was walking by the Sea of Galilee, He saw two brothers, Peter and Andrew casting a net into the sea for they were fishermen. Jesus said to **"Come, follow Me, and I will make you fishers of men!"**

They must have felt that Jesus was a special Person, so they left their nets and followed Him. As they moved on, Jesus called others to follow Him as well until He had twelve followers who were called His disciples. You can read all about this in the Gospels as well, so please take your Bible and read all about it, showing how Jesus chose His twelve disciples.

Thus, Jesus began His ministry as the Messiah, the Promised One, the Saviour of the World, fulfilling the very first promise of God to Adam and Eve, after they had **chosen** to follow the Serpent, Lucifer, instead of the Lord God, the Creator!

At the very beginning of this whole sad, but wonderful story, the Father, Son and Holy Spirit had this plan already in place, to offer once more to Adam and Eve. Not only to Adam and Eve but to all people who would come after them, right up to "the time of the end", the time of you and me, to anyone who would **choose** to accept the amazing love of God.

The following short story illustrates clearly our God-given **FREEWILL**, and our freedom to make **CHOICES.** We can **choose** to accept or reject God's love and the loving plan He has put in place at such a high price, to offer salvation to all mankind.

George Vandeman recounts this story of a man who was angry with God for the tragic loss of his wife and child some time before.

He was successful in rescuing a young orphan boy one day, from a burning building and decided to try to adopt the lad as his own.

Christian neighbours were not sure this was a good plan to place this boy into the home of someone who was not a believer, and who was blaming God for the loss of his own wife and child.

His hand had been badly burnt while rescuing the lad from the fire, leaving his hand severely scarred. While his application was being considered, as his final argument, he held up his hand for all to see, and the court deemed him worthy, and granted him custody of Bobby.

He really loved Bobby, and the little fellow never tired of hearing the story of how his father had rescued him from the burning building.

One day his father took his boy with him to see a special art display. Bobby was particularly interested in a painting of Jesus reproving Thomas for his unbelief, and holding out His scarred hand.

"Please tell me the story of that picture Daddy."

His father said, "No, not that one."

Bobby said, "Why not Daddy?"

"Because I don't believe it," was his father's reply.

"But you tell me the story of Jack the Giant Killer, and surely you don't believe that!"

So his father told him the story.

Bobby said, "It's like you and me Daddy. It wasn't nice for Thomas not to believe after that man died for him. What if they told me how you saved me from that terrible fire, and I said I didn't believe it?"

The father could not deny the logic of that little child. He had used his own scarred hand, to show his love for this child. How could he continue to deny the story of the Man who died for <u>him</u>, not only showing His scarred hands, but His feet and side as well? How could he keep saying Jesus didn't do it?

The demonstration of God's love at Calvary, is the mightiest evidence of all that GOD is LOVE. The scarred hands, feet and side of Jesus, will ever be there to remind us of the battle between God and Lucifer, throughout the ceaseless ages of eternity! Jesus Christ, His Heavenly Father, and His Holy Spirit had the victory when Jesus died there on Skull Hill, and cried out,

<u>**"IT IS FINISHED"**</u>, John 19:30

Another painting by a talented artist, of the Crucifixion scene.

What was **"FINISHED"**? Type had met antitype. The ceremonial sacrifices had met their fulfilment. The wages of sin were **PAID IN FULL**, by the sinless Son of God. Salvation is available to all who **CHOOSE** to accept Jesus as their Saviour from sin and eternal death.

Lucifer and his followers will eventually cease to exist! Never more will sin be allowed to raise its ugly head!

Many people today don't believe God and His love for us all, when they see the atrocities and horrible crimes that have happened in the past, since the time Cain killed his brother Abel. The murder of innocent babies by Herod; the millions of innocent people who have lost their lives in many wars; the persecution and hate that is still going on in our sad old world, all demonstrate the works of Satan and his followers.

How can we believe God is love when He allows all this horrible stuff to keep happening, as is being reported on the news everyday now? Why doesn't God do something?

Just consider what the Heavenly Angels, and all God's creation throughout the universe, would have thought and believed, if Almighty God had used His power to wipe out Lucifer and his followers when the war began in heaven? Why did He allow all this sin and suffering, when He could have erased it all with just one Word! **"He just has to speak, and it is done. He commands and it stands fast!"** Psalm 33:9

Every being would be afraid of God and wondering if they unknowingly did something that God didn't like that they would be also wiped out of existence! That would be a God of **FORCE** and not a God of **LOVE**!

God chose to demonstrate that He is not a God of **Force**. He is truly a God of **Love** and is **"not willing that any should perish!"** 2 Peter 3:9

What is the most frequently asked question ….**"If He is a God of LOVE, why doesn't He do something?"**

Please forgive me for repeating myself….

Because God is a God of LOVE, never again will He allow any being or anything to arise which is not of LOVE. He will be perfectly justified in erasing that being or thing, to protect His Kingdom, and every intelligent being, the heavenly hosts of angels, and all His creation will say, "Amen", and thank God for protecting us from ever again witnessing the ugliness of sin throughout the ceaseless ages of eternity.

The only reminder of what sin does will be the marks of the Crucifixion in the hands and feet and side of the sinless Son of God, Who died in our stead, to give all of us the opportunity to use our FREEWILL to CHOOSE to accept or reject the offer of salvation and eternal life with God in a totally recreated earth.

He has determined a period of time for this demonstration. It has been going on **for nearly six thousand years.** We haven't seen the worst of it yet, according to the Word of God. There is yet to be a **"time of trouble such as never was since there was a nation."** Daniel 12, and Jesus' own words as in Matthew 24.

"A thousand years is but a day with the Lord." 2 Peter 3:8. Six thousand years is but six days with the Lord! Could it be that we are nearing the end of this **"six days"** with all its sin, suffering and death?

Could it be that the seventh day, the seventh thousand years, will be the Sabbath of the Lord? Could it be that all the offspring of the Saviour will enjoy a thousand years, <u>the seventh day Sabbath,</u> with the Lord in Heaven?

The devil, Satan, is bound for that thousand years because the rest of the dead lived not till the thousand years were finished. This is recorded in God's Word. There will be no one alive for those thousand years for Satan and his evil angels to tempt, and cause more sin, and suffering and death!

Check with I Thessalonians 4:16-18. Also, see Revelation 20:1-6.

The story doesn't finish there. There is good news to follow which His saved ones will enjoy forever. Jesus says plainly in John 14: 1-3,

"Let not your hearts be troubled: ye believe in God, believe also in Me. In my Father's house are many mansions: if it were not so, I would have told you. And if I go and prepare a place for you, I will come again, and receive you unto Myself; that where I am there ye may be also."

That sounds like a very loving promise to me, and something to look forward to, for all who **choose** to accept His love! **Even the animals agree and know God's love!**

Even the animals agree, it's all about LOVE!

CHAPTER 21

THE GREAT DECEIVER

In the book of Revelation, written by the disciple John, we find the wonderful end of this whole demonstration of the love of God.

The "blessed hope" of the seed of the woman; the "blessed hope" of all the followers of God since Adam and Eve. The "blessed hope" is an "endless hope", instead of a "hopeless end!"

The whole story is vividly and clearly told in the final chapters of this book revealing how the demonstration ends! It reveals the end of the battle between the empire of Lucifer based on **Force,** and the beginning of the triumphant everlasting empire, God's empire of **Love!**

As we near the end of this world, Satan knows he has but a short time left and is **"going about as a roaring lion, seeking whom he may devour".** (1 Peter 5:8)

He is a liar, and **"the father of lies".** (John 8:44). He has many lies he has promulgated upon humanity, which have been accepted by so many as Truth. Even Christian churches have accepted his lies! One of these lies is about what happens when we die.

Here is a study I have put together on this subject which will be very important to understand.

<u>Life After Death—What Does the BIBLE say?</u>

1.　　**Death is like a sleep in an unconscious state until the resurrection. John 11:11-14**

2.　　**The devil is masquerading as the dead to deceive people. He is a liar. John 8:44**

3.　　**To accept and follow Christ is the only way to have the hope of the resurrection.**

 J.B.Phillips, who translated the Bible into modern English, was sitting in his home one day when suddenly, what looked like C.S.Lewis, the famous Christian philosopher, who had died some time before, appeared before him and then disappeared.

Wondering what was going on, Phillips visited another Christian leader, who simply said,

"This sort of thing is happening all the time, JB!"

My own mother-in-law lost her youngest daughter in a car accident many years ago. One day she saw what looked like her daughter appear in front of her. She said "No! It can't be! It isn't!" and the thing vanished.

These "appearances" can be multiplied over and over. The arch deceiver is constantly trying to have people believe that the dead are NOT dead!

In the very beginning, when God said to our first parents, **"But of the tree of the knowledge of good and evil, thou shalt not eat of it: for in the day that thou eatest thereof, <u>thou shalt surely die</u>." Genesis 2:17**

In the very next chapter 3: 4,5, we have **"the serpent said unto the woman, <u>Ye shall NOT surely die."</u>**

Here we have the very first lie! No wonder Jesus said what He did in John 8:44.

<u>**John 8:44 says,**</u> **" Ye are of your father the devil, and the lusts of your father ye will do. He was a murderer from the beginning, and abode not in the truth, because there is no truth in him. When he speaketh a lie, he speaketh of his own: for he is a liar, and the father of it."**

Ever since then Satan, that old serpent the devil, (Rev. 12:9) has been deceiving the whole world, perpetuating that original lie! Most of the world and the churches in general have accepted this lie!

It is becoming more and more popular every day, to try to contact the dead, through spirit mediums, channelers, witches and wizards, séances, tarot cards, palm reading, star signs, near death experiences, UFOs and on and on. Satan is using the media in a mighty way to promote his lie, and there's not a day goes by that we don't see this lie being promoted somewhere, even in the churches!

All of mankind has to face death someday, and we all want to know what is "on the other side". It is the imperial question we all need answers for. The answers are right there in Scripture if we will just study it for ourselves.

On a tombstone in Virginia, USA, is the following inscription:

"Stop my friend, as you go by.

As you are, so once was I.

As I am now, you soon shall be--

So, prepare yourself to follow me."

A young boy not content with this, scrawled underneath,

"To follow you I am not content,

Until I know just where you went."

So, where do the dead go at death?

Some believe if they are good, they go to Heaven. If they are bad, they go to Hell!

Others say Purgatory—Eastern Religions say --Re-incarnation.

Is there conscious life after death? Can we really contact the dead? Is there any hope beyond the Grave? Let's look at the Bible where we find the answers……..

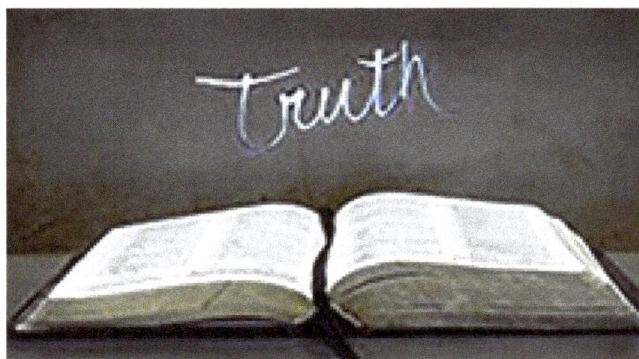

Let's see what our LOVING Heavenly Father says!

CHAPTER 22

LIFE AFTER DEATH

Let's begin in Revelation where Jesus said,

"I am He Who lives, and was dead, and behold, I am alive forevermore. Amen. And I have the keys of Hades (the Grave), and of Death." Rev 1:18

There **is** life after death! There **is** hope beyond tomorrow! It is because Jesus now has power over death and the grave!

Let's look at a wonderful story in John 11. Jesus was doing what He did best—healing broken lives and hearts, when a man sent from Martha and Mary burst through the crowd with a cryptic message---"Your friend Lazarus is sick!"

<u>John 11:5,6</u> says, **"Now Jesus loved Martha, and her sister, and Lazarus. So when He heard that he was sick, He stayed two more days in the place where He was."**

It is often hard to understand God's ways, and His plans. He doesn't always work to our schedules and expectations. But the Bible says:

<u>Romans 8:28</u> , **"And we know that all things work together for good to them that love God, to them who are the called according to his purpose."**

So, **FOUR** days later Jesus turned up in the town of Bethany where Martha and Mary lived. And when He did, the Bible says, **"Jesus wept." John 11:35**

God understands when we lose our loved ones, and He hasn't changed. He cares about you and your loved ones who have passed away, or who are right now **"walking through the valley of the shadow of death." Ps 23.**

Now Martha said to Jesus, **"Lord, if You had been here, my brother would not have died." John 11:21**

At death, we blame someone, often ourselves. Many times, we blame the person who died. But above all we blame God, and we want to know why especially, if the death is premature. It is part of the grief process, and God understands our questions and even our anger at Him.

Jesus said to her, **"Your brother will rise again."**

Martha said, **"I know that he will rise again in the resurrection at the last day."**

Jesus said to her, **"I am the Resurrection and the Life. He who believes in Me, though he may die, he shall live. And whoever lives and believes in Me shall never die. Do you believe this?"** **(John 11: 23-26)**

"NEVER DIE?" "What do you mean? Lazarus believed in You, and he is dead! I don't understand!" Can you imagine Martha's dilemma?

Albert Barnes explains this statement well. He says, **"They shall never come into <u>eternal</u> death."** In the Greek it says, **"Shall by no means die forever."** They won't remain dead forever.

Now let's go back to where Jesus was when He received the message, that Lazarus was sick. After two days, Jesus said,

"Our friend Lazarus sleeps, but I go that I may wake him up."

Then His disciples said. **"Lord, if he sleeps, he will get well."**

However, Jesus spoke of his death, but <u>they</u> thought that He was speaking about taking rest in sleep.

Then Jesus said to them plainly, **"Lazarus is dead!"** (John 11: 11-14)

Jesus clearly calls death a sleep, as does the rest of the Bible—God's Holy Word.

But why does God's Word call death a sleep?

Ecclesiastes 9:5, 6, "For the living know that they will die; but the dead know nothing. And they have no more reward, for the memory of them is forgotten. Also, their love, their hatred, and their envy have now perished. Nevermore will they have a share in anything done under the sun."

Job 14: 14,21, "If a man dies.......his sons come to honour, and he does not know it; they are brought low, and he does not perceive it."

Death is likened to a deep sleep because they know nothing in death—absolutely nothing!

You and I know what it's like. You lay your head on the pillow and the next thing you know the old alarm clock is ringing in your ear. When you sleep well, you have no sense of time or of anything that is going on around you. You know nothing. That's why criminals usually work in the night-- when people are asleep or 'dead to the world' as we often say!

The Bible says death is like that! But someone says, "Don't our loved ones go to heaven at death?"

Now that would be a comforting thought but let us see what the Bible says about our loved ones.

In **Psalm 115:17** we read:

"The dead do not praise the LORD, nor any who go down into silence."

When Peter was preaching on the Day of Pentecost, notice carefully what he said:

"Men and brethren, let me speak freely to you of the patriarch David, that he is both dead and buried, and his tomb is with us to this day." Acts 2:29

You can still visit the tomb of David in Jerusalem today.

Let me ask a question of you. How many of you think David will be in heaven?

Now I know David did some very bad things, but the Bible says he repented and was forgiven by God's amazing Grace and the New Testament Book of Hebrews tells us he was one of the great heroes of faith.

But notice what Peter added: **"For David did NOT ascend into the heavens…" Acts 2:34.**

Clearly, even in Peter's time, David was not yet in heaven!

Let's go to the 11th chapter of Hebrews, which is called the Faith Chapter. It mentions all the great people of faith like Abel, Noah, and Abraham. Speaking of all these people the Bible says:

"But now they desire a better, that is, a heavenly country… for He has prepared a city for them…..and all these ….did not receive the promise. God having provided something better for us, that they should not be made perfect apart from us." Hebrews 11: 16, 39.

Clearly, none of them are in heaven at this point in time. They are all waiting till we all go there together, on resurrection day.

This agrees with the rest of Scripture. Job said:

"So man lies down and does not rise. Till the heavens are no more, they will not awake, nor be roused from their sleep." Job 14: 12

So when will they wake up from their sleep? The apostle Paul gives us the answer in **1 Thessalonians 4: 13-18**

"But I do not want you to be ignorant, brethren, concerning those who have fallen asleep, lest you sorrow as others who have no hope…..For the Lord Himself shall descend from heaven with a shout, with the voice of the archangel, and with the trumpet of God. And the dead in Christ will rise first. Then we who are alive and remain shall be caught up together with them in the clouds to meet the Lord in the air. And so shall we ever be with the Lord. Therefore comfort one another with these words."

How their hearts must have been comforted with these words!

They would see their loved ones again, for they will be sleeping till Jesus awakes them from their sleep when He returns.

What a glorious and fantastic day that will be when Jesus returns. That is when the dead will be woken out of their sleep! Just imagine the re-unions that will take place on that day!

The Second Coming of Jesus is the day to wake those who sleep in Jesus to life, according to God's Holy Word. That is the day the faithful will meet Jesus, with their faithful loved ones who may be still living when He returns.

According to the Bible, the dead friends of Jesus do **NOT** meet Him at death. They meet Him **WITH** their loved ones, who may still be alive WHEN He returns, **NOT** before. There is no point in Paul telling them they will meet Jesus when He returns, if they have already met Him in heaven at death!

This is why Paul said to comfort each other with THESE words; not by saying the dead are now already with the Lord in heaven.

Isn't it more comforting to think of us all going to meet Jesus together, rather than some of us being down here, and some of us being up there watching our loved ones, friends, and all people still alive here, getting into all sorts of difficulties, disease, sin, murders, cruelty and death?

To me, those who are resting, and those who are still alive when Jesus returns, going to meet our Saviour Jesus and our Heavenly Father **together** is a much more loving plan of our loving God!

Again, it really is all about LOVE!

CHAPTER 23

A VERY COMMON BELIEF

But someone says, "Isn't the soul immortal?"

The words **SOUL** and **SPIRIT** are mentioned around 1600 times in the Bible, **but NEVER as immortal!**

There is no such thing in the Bible as an "immortal soul". **Only God is immortal!**

Speaking of God, Paul declared,

"……He who is the blessed and only Potentate, the King of Kings and Lord of Lords, Who <u>alone</u> has immortality……." 1Timothy 6: 15,16. Notice the word **"ALONE"**. Only God has immortality! No one else has it yet!

This brings us to a very important question---**What is a soul?**

We need to go back to the book of beginnings—Genesis—to the creation of humans. Let's look at the King James Version:

Genesis 2:7 "And the LORD God formed man of the dust of the ground, and breathed into his nostrils the breath of life, and man became a living soul."

To simplify the action let's do some simple math:

Dust of the ground + Breath of Life from God = Living Soul.

Notice that man BECAME a Living Soul. God did NOT put a Soul IN man; rather he BECAME a living soul.

Dust plus Breath makes a Living Soul, or a Living Being as it says in the NKJV. Or, the Elements of the earth plus Breath of Life from God make a Living Being.

The Bible informs us that there is no soul without a body—the elements. A Living Soul simply means a Living Being—a Living Person.

Thus, another word for "soul" in the Bible is "person" or "life".

Notice how the following verse in Ezekiel 18: 4 NKJV puts it:

"The soul who sins shall die."

The Good News translation says: **"The person** who sins is the one who will die."

The Living Bible translation says: It is for **a man's** own sins that he will die."

The soul is the entire person, and must have a body to be a soul, according to God's Word. **God did not put a soul IN man—he BECAME a soul.** Death is simply creation in reverse.

Ecclesiastes 12:7 **"Then the dust will return to the earth as it was, And the spirit will return to God Who gave it."**

The word translated "spirit" is from the Hebrew *"ruach"* which means "breath" or "wind".

This is brought out in the Good News Bible translation of this verse:

"Our bodies will return to the dust of the earth, and the breath of life will go back to God, Who gave it to us." (Ecclesiastes 12:7)

In the Bible the Spirit and Soul are different—they are <u>not</u> the same thing.

Remember we saw that God BREATHED Breath or Spirit into Man, and man BECAME a Living Soul or Person. At death the body or person goes back to dust. The spirit or breath of life from God goes back to God.

Men of science today can replicate a wheat seed so that it is identical with its look alike, but there is a huge difference between the two. Plant both seeds, and only one will grow—the one which had LIFE from God embedded in it. Scientists cannot supply that LIFE FORCE which only comes from the Creator. He alone is able to give Life to all his Creation. When we lose that life force at death, we are truly DEAD!

The Bible clearly shows that Breath and the Spirit are the same thing.

In the NKJV translation **Job 27: 3** says, **"As long as my breath is in me, and the breath of God is in my nostrils…."**

In the KJV it reads, **"As long as my breath is in me, and the <u>spirit of God is in my nostrils …</u>" Job 27:3**

The reason for this is that the Hebrew word here—*ruach*—means both breath and spirit. So you can see that breath and spirit are the same. No one believes that some ghostly thing lives in our noses. No, the "spirit" here means "breath", "wind", or "air".

Just as God breathed spirit or breath, (energy of life), into man at creation, so it returns to Him at death.

This is why the New Testament says, **"For as the body without the spirit is dead…."** James 2:26

So, James is saying, a living person minus the spirit is a corpse. Mathematically it can be expressed as a simple equation: **body - breath = dead corpse.**

It can be illustrated also using a light bulb. Pass electricity through it and we have light. Take away that energy and the light goes out!

The bulb is like the Body. Add breath or Energy from God, and you have a Living Person or Light. Take away the Energy from God, and all you have left is a bulb. The light has gone out.

The person ceases to exist.

Well, will we ever be immortal? Absolutely, if we are faithful!

The Bible says, in 1 Corinthians 15:52-54

"For the trumpet will sound, and the dead will be raised incorruptible, and we shall be changed. For this corruptible must <u>put on</u> incorruption, and this mortal must <u>put on</u> immortality…. then shall be brought to pass the saying that is written: 'Death is swallowed up in victory."

You will notice that Immortality is **"PUT ON"** at Christ's return—**NOT** before.

So where did the teaching of the immortal soul come from, and how did it become part of so-called Christianity?

Tertullian, one of the early church fathers living after the time of the Bible, between 160-225AD said,

<u>"I may use, therefore, the opinion of PLATO, when he declares, 'Every soul is immortal.'"</u>

(Tertullian, *On the Resurrection of the Flesh, Chapter III; Anti-Nicene Fathers*, Vol III , p. 202) So….it came from Plato, who was a Pagan Greek Philosopher. Pagan Greek Philosophy taught that the soul is immortal.

The body they said was like a house. At death the body became crumbled, allowing the spirit or soul to leave the body and go elsewhere.

The Word of God—the Bible, reveals that the real origins of this belief came from a deceiving serpent at the beginning of this world. Satan is the Father of Lies, and it is amazing how so many, even professed Christians, have swallowed his lie, "hook line and sinker!"

When God made man, He warned:

"Of every tree of the garden you may freely eat; but of the tree of the knowledge of good and evil you shall not eat, for in the day that you eat of it you shall surely die." Genesis 2:16,17

In plain English…. **"Adam and Eve, if you eat of this tree, you will die!"**

But in total contradiction to God, Satan through the snake, as a medium, said,

"You will NOT surely die." Genesis 3:4. And he is still today convincing millions of every culture, this Satanic belief, that something lives on after death—that you really don't die! Your spirit or soul continues living somewhere! This is nothing other than the spurious lie of the Devil.

So, why did Satan formulate the belief of an immortal soul—a belief that is found globally in nearly every religion—both Christian and Non-Christian?

He deceives to take people to eternal destruction—that is his prime objective. Remember what Jesus said in John 8:44

"Ye are of *your* father the devil, and the lusts of your father ye will do<u>. He was a murderer from the beginning, and abode not in the truth, because there is no truth in him. When he speaketh a lie, he speaketh of his own: for he is a liar, and the father of it."</u>

What about those "out of body experiences", that so many people have—surely, they are real! Just remember that they contradict this Book, God's Holy Word, which says,

"For the living know that they shall die, <u>but the dead know not anything</u>." Ecclesiastes 9:5

Not long ago, TIME Magazine ran a feature article on "near death" or "out of body experiences" and pointed out that near death there are altered states of consciousness, which cause people to hallucinate.

And the BBC News reported on August 23, 2007, that scientists are able to generate "out of body experiences" on people who are very much alive.

Then, what about all those amazing stories of reincarnated lives, where people tell us that in a previous life, they were Mozart or Napoleon Bonaparte or some other person!

Again, just remember that they contradict this Book, the Bible, which says,

"For the living know that they will die; but the dead know nothing...." Ecclesiastes 9:5

"And as it is appointed for men <u>to die once</u>, but after this the judgment..."Hebrews 9:27

We die ONCE according to the Bible. It is totally opposed to the idea of some sort of recycling of the soul.

Here's a couple of thoughts to set you thinking:

"Is it better to be born twice and die once, or to be born once and die twice!"

Then there is Channelling or Spiritualism! So, what about reports of people seeing or speaking to the dead? It is becoming more and more common every day. What is going on?

Remember that we need to see things as God sees them—to look behind the scenes!

"It is NOT the dead who are communicating with you."

It may look and sound like your loved one. They may even say things that only you and they know about. But it is not the dead for the Bible declares categorically,

"For the living know that they shall die, but the dead know not anything. And they have no more reward, for their memory is forgotten.

Also, their love, their hatred, and their envy have now perished. Nevermore will they have a share in anything that is done under the sun." Ecclesiastes 9:5,6

If the dead know nothing, how can they be talking with you? The Bible is clear—they have no more involvement with us who are alive---**until Jesus comes!**

The precious Word of God helps to protect us from the lies of Satan. He has given us His Holy Scriptures to protect us from Satan's lies, because He loves us all as His special creation, made in His image. So, to read his Word to understand His Truth, is the only way to recognise Satan's lies!

Once more, it's all about Truth and LOVE!

CHAPTER 24

THE RICH MAN AND LAZARUS

What about the story Jesus told of the Rich Man and Lazarus? Doesn't that show we go to heaven or hell when we die?

Even in Jesus' day Satan had brought in so many lies over that first 4000 years. Paganism was rife in many areas of the world, and the Jews had embraced a number of these pagan ideas, and Jesus used one of these prevailing beliefs to show the Truth that riches cannot earn you a ticket to heaven, and that when a person dies their opportunity for salvation has passed.

Jesus framed His parable, so as to teach important Truths, through their preconceived opinions. Many of the Jews believed the heathen idea of a conscious state of man in death. This is quite contrary to the teaching of Scripture as we have already seen.

The story is found in Luke 16: 19-31.

We need to answer some very important questions here:

1.   Was the poor beggar with all his rags and sores literally carried by the angels to Abraham's bosom? **That is not taught in Scripture!**

2.   Did the rich man come back to life after he was dead and buried in hell to be able to speak to God? **Scripture does NOT support this idea.**

3.   Does this story negate all the rest of Scripture? **Definitely not. It was a simple story showing the foolishness and error of such beliefs.**

There were many other pagan ideas and beliefs prevalent as well.

Another prevailing lie of the day was espoused even by a sect of the Jewish Leaders called the Sadducees, who believed that there would be NO RESURRECTION! That's why they were **Sad You See!**

And what about haunted houses?

Again, it is NOT the dead, for the Bible clearly says,

"So he who goes down to the grave does not come up. <u>He shall never return to his house,</u> nor shall his place know him anymore." Job 7: 9,10

So, whoever it is, the Bible says clearly, **IT IS NOT THE DEAD!** Well, who is it?

Have you noticed that there is real enmity between Christ and Satan. It has been going on since there was war in heaven. See Revelation 12. The Bible reveals a Final Battle for Global Worship or Allegiance.

The Bible also reveals those who are doing these things.

"For they are the spirits of demons, performing signs…." Revelation 16:14

This is why the Bible warns us not to try to contact the dead.

"There shall not be found among you anyone who…practices witchcraft…or a medium, or a spiritist, or one who calls up the dead. For all who do these things are an abomination to the LORD…." Deuteronomy 18: 10-12

Why does the Bible warn us this way?

Because, when we do these things, we are really contacting evil spirits or Satan and his angels who were cast out of heaven when they rebelled against God. Those who do these things are really contacting God's enemies, and as the saying goes, "You can't have your bottom on two horses at the same time!"

How diabolical is the Devil? At our weakest and most vulnerable times in life—the death of a loved one—he moves in with his lies. It doesn't get more despicable than that!

Let's go back to John 11. And so, four days too late Jesus walked into the town of Bethany.

They took Him to the tomb, and He said, **"Roll away the stone!"**

Standing in front of the tomb, He called out, **"Lazarus, come forth!"**

Notice He did not say, Lazarus come down or Lazarus come up!

Lazarus came forth out of the tomb because Jesus has Power over Death.

I often wonder why Jesus addressed Lazarus personally. Why didn't He just say, "Come forth!"? Someone has suggested that if He had just said "Come forth!" all those who had ever lived would have arisen. He will keep that command for His return, and what a day that will be, **"when all that are in the graves shall hear His Voice and shall arise."** John 5: 25

Matthew 24: 30, 31 **"And then shall appear the sign of the Son of man in heaven: and then shall all the tribes of the earth mourn, and they shall see the Son of man coming in the clouds of heaven with power and great glory. And he shall send his angels with a great sound of a trumpet, and they shall gather together his elect from the four winds, from one end of heaven to the other."**

1Thess. 4:16, 17 **"For the Lord himself shall descend from heaven with a shout, with the voice of the archangel, and with the trump of God: and the dead in Christ shall rise first: then we who are alive and remain shall be caught up in the clouds to meet the Lord in the air, and so shall we ever be with the Lord."**

Rev 20:13 **"And the sea gave up the dead which were in it; and death and hell delivered up the dead which were in them: and they were judged every man according to their works."**

With Lazarus, dead for four days, and his body already decomposing, we see in reality, a re-play of Adam's Creation.

Where was the dust of the earth?   In the tomb!

Where was the Breath of Life?   In Jesus!

Remember Jesus' Words,

"I am the resurrection and the Life. He who believes in Me, though he may die, he shall live." John 11:35

Right there, in those words of hope, are the **TWO** necessary ingredients for having Life after Death.

1.   **There must be a Resurrection.**

2.   **There must be a Belief in Jesus.**

Because Lazarus had believed in Jesus, at Jesus' voice the two came together—the Life or Spirit or Breath that is in Jesus our Creator, and the decomposing body of Lazarus in the tomb—and Lazarus came to life—a living soul!

There is no life after death without a Resurrection at Christ's return, and to live after death one must believe in Jesus.

If we die believing in Jesus, we too, like Lazarus, will rise from the dead when Jesus comes again and calls us to come forth.

And what is even better, it will be a life with Jesus forever.

The thief on the cross, believed in Him. He said,

"Lord, remember me when You come into Your Kingdom." Luke 23:42

And Jesus responded,

"Assuredly, I say to you, today you will be with Me in Paradise." Luke 23:43

What is going on here?? It looks as if the thief would be in Paradise that very day! Does it undo everything we have learnt so far?

What you may not realize is that when the Bible was written, there were no punctuation marks in it. There weren't even any spaces between the words if you check on some of the old manuscripts of the Bible. Punctuation marks were placed there at a later time, and those who did it got it wrong in this instance.

To be in harmony with the rest of Scripture it should read:

"Assuredly, I say to you today, you will be with Me in Paradise." Luke 23:43.

Jesus was saying to him, 'Today, when all looks lost for you and Me, Today, I am telling you, you will be with Me in Paradise.'

How do we know this? Because Jesus did not go to Paradise that day. Even on the resurrection morning, very early Sunday, Jesus told Mary not to touch Him as He had not yet ascended to the Father in heaven.

What an incredible difference a bit of punctuation can make!

A story is told of a lady on holiday in Europe from America many years ago. She saw a lovely fur coat, that she took a fancy to, and sent a telegram to her husband asking if she could buy it as it was quite expensive.

The husband sent her his reply:

"NO PRICE TOO DEAR."

The wife thought, "Isn't he sweet!" and bought the coat.

When she came home wearing the expensive fur coat, the husband was quite surprised to put it mildly.

"Didn't I send you a telegram saying, **"NO. PRICE TOO DEAR"**.

Somehow the full stop had got lost in sending the telegram.

It just goes to show how important punctuation can be.

Wellington had fought Napoleon at the Battle of Waterloo.

The message of the outcome of the battle was taken across the English Channel and was relayed to London by Semaphore which was a method used in those days of sending messages by the waving of flags.

The message was being sent: **"WELLINGTON DEFEATED…"** when an English fog interrupted the full message, and those two words were sent on as the full message to London. Everyone thought Wellington had been defeated. Gloom settled over London with everyone believing Napoleon had won.

However, as the sun rose later in the day dispersing the fog, the message was able to be completed:

"WELLINGTON DEFEATED THE ENEMY!"

What a difference the full message made! Now gloom was turned into joy!

Two thousand years ago on that fearful Friday, it looked like the message was….

"JESUS DEFEATED…."

But on Sunday morning, when Jesus came forth from the tomb triumphant, the message was very clear!

"JESUS DEFEATED DEATH."

And the Good News is: Jesus is coming again to raise His faithful people who have died, to LIFE ETERNAL, and His faithful ones who are alive and remain will be changed in a moment, in the twinkling of an eye!

See 1 Corinthians 15: 51-58.

Is there life after death? There is indeed for those who have chosen to give their lives and hearts to Jesus, and when He returns as King of Kings, with the keys of Hell and Death, they will awake from sleep, and experience the wonderful transformation as described in Corinthians. Then will be brought to pass the saying, **"O Death, where is your sting? O Grave, where is thy victory?"**

1 Corinthians 15: 55-57

Have you put your trust in Jesus? Have you given Him your heart and life, so that He can make you immortal when He returns?

What a wonderful loving God we serve! All praise and adoration to His Name! He is indeed a God of **LOVE**! Please join with me in accepting this most loving gift!

Jesus raised Lazarus back to life. He dearly LOVED Lazarus and his sisters.

CHAPTER 25

TWO IMPORTANT TRUTHS

It should be pointed out that there are two resurrections mentioned in Scripture:

(1) The Resurrection of Life, and

(2) The Resurrection of Damnation.

"Marvel not at this: for the hour is coming, in the which all that are in the graves shall hear his voice and shall come forth; they that have done good, unto (1) the resurrection of life; and they that have done evil, unto (2) the resurrection of damnation." (John 5:28,29).

Both the righteous and the wicked, will be resurrected to life. However, **the resurrection of the wicked will be _after_ the thousand years.** (during which time the righteous will sit on thrones, as they are involved in the judgment). Although the wicked will be resurrected, it will only be temporary, or for a limited time.

"And I saw thrones, and *they sat upon them,* **and judgment was given unto them: and [I saw] the souls of them that were beheaded for the witness of Jesus, and for the word of God, and which had not worshipped the beast, neither his image, neither had received [his] mark upon their foreheads, or in their hands; and they** *lived and reigned with Christ a thousand years.* **But** *the rest of the dead* **(i.e., the wicked, who will be raised to life after the thousand years)** *lived not again until the thousand years were finished"* (Revelation 20:4,5). **So, repeating the matter, the righteous will be resurrected when Jesus returns, before the thousand years (the millennium), but the wicked will not be resurrected until after the thousand years:**

"For the Lord himself shall descend from heaven with a shout, with the voice of the arch-angel, and with the trump of God: and *the dead in Christ shall rise first:* **Then we which are alive and remain shall be caught up together with them in the clouds, to meet the Lord in the air: and so shall we ever be with the Lord. Wherefore comfort one another with these words"** (1 Thessalonians 4:16-18).

At the first resurrection, the resurrected righteous, along with those who do not see death (those **"which are alive and remain"**), will be caught up into the air together, and be transported with Jesus to heaven, where they will be involved in the judgment during the thousand years: **"Let not your heart be troubled: ye believe in God, believe also in me. In my Father's house are many mansions: if it were not so, I would have told you. I go to prepare a place for you. And if I go and prepare a place for you, I will come again and receive you unto myself; that** *where I am, there ye may be also".* (John 14:1-3).

Jesus is in heaven now and will return to take the righteous to heaven, so that where He is, they (the righteous) can be there also.

After the thousand years in heaven, God and His people will return to this earth with the holy city, New Jerusalem: **"And I John saw the holy city, new Jerusalem, coming down from God out of heaven, prepared as a bride adorned for her husband"**. (Revelation 21:2).

At that time, at the end of the thousand years, the resurrected wicked, marshalled together by Satan, will surround the saints who are in the New Jerusalem; but fire will come from God out of heaven and devour them: **"And when the thousand years are expired, Satan shall be loosed out of his prison, And shall go out to deceive the nations which are in the four quarters of the earth, Gog and Magog, to gather them together to battle: the number of whom [is] as the sand of the sea. And they went up on the breadth of the earth, and compassed** (i.e. "surrounded") **the camp of the saints about, and the beloved city: and fire came down from God out of heaven and devoured them"**. (Revelation 20: 7-9).

<u>The wicked will consume away into smoke, as if they had never existed</u>. As someone might say of total destruction, "They have gone up in smoke." They will be reduced to dust and ashes:

"But *the wicked shall perish,* and the enemies of the LORD shall be *as the fat of lambs:* they shall consume; *into smoke shall they consume away"*. (Psalm 37:20).

"For behold, the day cometh, that shall burn as an oven; and *all the proud,* yea, and all that do wickedly, *shall be stubble:* and the day that cometh shall burn them up, saith the LORD of hosts, that *it shall leave them neither root nor branch, and ye shall tread down the wicked; for they shall be ashes under the soles of your feet in the day that I shall do this, saith the LORD of hosts"*. (Malachi 4:1,3).

Incidentally, have you ever seen an apple that has perished? It slowly decays, and in the end turns back to dust, which can be blown away in the wind. The word "perish" occurs in probably the most well-known verse in Scripture:

John 3:16 -17 **"For God so loved the world, that he gave his only begotten Son, that whosoever believeth in him *should not perish,* but have everlasting life." According to this verse, there are two alternatives: Either (1) To have *everlasting life,* or (2) *to* <u>perish</u>. It seems to me that, if people were to burn in hellfire forever and ever without end, they would have everlasting life in hellfire; and that is <u>*not perishing.*</u>**

The ugliest picture of God engineered by the enemy of God, Satan, is that those who don't serve God and don't accept His offer of salvation, will burn in hellfire throughout eternity! Can you imagine anyone hearing and believing that picture of our loving God, would want to live with Him, and serve Him as they watch their loved ones, their wives, their children, or their friends who did not accept Him, burning in hellfire forever, throughout all eternity!?

The idea of eternally burning torture in hell, cannot be sustained from a careful study of God's Word. By early New Testament times, Greek philosophy was intertwined with the Middle Eastern mind. There were well-known mythical stories which Jesus used to emphasise a point, not to support bad theology. One such story was of the Rich Man and Lazarus (see Luke 16:19-31), a story that, if literally true, would support the idea of an eternally burning hellfire of torture for the wicked. However, Jesus used this parable (or Greek story) to emphasise a point that, even if someone should come back from the dead, it would be impossible to save some who **choose** to reject His loving offer of salvation!

After the final destruction of Satan, the evil angels and the wicked, the saints will then live on the earth made new with God forever and ever. Death, tears and sorrow will be forever banished, and peace, harmony and love will reign supreme forever:

"And I heard a great voice out of heaven saying, Behold, the tabernacle of God is with men, and he will dwell with them, and they shall be his people, and God himself shall be with them, and be their God. And God shall wipe away all tears from their eyes; and there shall be no more death, neither sorrow, nor crying, neither shall there be any more pain: for the former things are passed away" (Revelation 21:3,4).

There may seem to be some "scary" passages in Scripture, and some may ask why anyone would want to serve a God Who will ultimately destroy anyone who rejects His ways. An easy answer to that is that God knows best. **He is a God of love, Who is not willing for any to perish".** 2 Peter 3:9; 1 Timothy 2:4

He wants everyone to live with Him throughout eternity. He sent His only Son to die for the sins of the world so that <u>all</u> might receive eternal life.

Perhaps someone thinks that, if they were God, they would have done things differently. The fact is that they are NOT God, and that God established things His way; it is not for us to question the way of God. As the Scripture says, **"I call heaven and earth to record this day against you, that I have set before you life and death, blessing and cursing: therefore, choose life, that both thou and thy seed may live".** (Deuteronomy 30:19).

Whether we receive eternal life or death is <u>our decision</u>. So, why not **choose** eternal life while we have the chance. There is nothing to lose! Won't you join with me and accept this gift of **LOVE**.

My prayer is that we will each accept God's love, and follow the decision of God's servant Joshua who said,

"And if it seem evil unto you to serve the LORD, CHOOSE you this day whom ye will serve; whether the gods which your fathers served that were on the other side of the flood, or the gods of the Amorites, in whose land ye dwell: _but as for me and my house, we will serve the LORD_" (Joshua 24:15).

True LOVE allows FREEDOM to CHOOSE!

CHAPTER 26

BROTHERLY LOVE

I'd like to share another wonderful example of true love about two brothers, which really touched my heart. It's called **"Praying Hands".**

Back in the fifteenth century, in a tiny village near Nuremberg, lived a family with eighteen children. Eighteen! In order merely to keep food on the table for this mob, the father and head of the household, a goldsmith by profession, worked almost eighteen hours a day at his trade and any other paying chore he could find in the neighbourhood, to keep food on the table for his wife and children.

Despite their seemingly hopeless condition, two of the father's older children had a dream. They both wanted to pursue their talent for art, but they knew full well that their father would never be financially able to send either of them to Nuremberg to study at the Academy.

After many long discussions at night in their crowded bed, the two boys finally worked out a pact. They would toss a coin. The loser would go down into the nearby mines and, with his earnings, support his brother while he attended the academy. Then, when that brother who won the toss completed his studies, in four years, he would support the other brother at the academy, either with sales of his artwork or, if necessary, also by labouring in the mines.

They tossed a coin one morning after church, and Albrecht Durer won the toss and went off to Nuremberg Academy. Albert went down into the dangerous mines and, for the next four years, financed his brother, whose work at the academy was almost an immediate sensation. Albrecht's etchings, his woodcuts, and his oils were far better than those of most of his professors, and by the time he graduated, he was beginning to earn considerable fees for his commissioned works.

When the young artist returned to his village, the Durer family held a festive dinner on their lawn to celebrate Albrecht's triumphant homecoming. After a long and memorable meal, punctuated with music and laughter, Albrecht rose from his honoured position at the head of the table to drink a toast to his beloved brother for the years of sacrifice that had enabled Albrecht to fulfil his ambition. His closing words were, "And now, Albert, blessed brother of mine, now it is your turn. Now you can go to Nuremberg to pursue your dream, and I will take care of you."

All heads turned in eager expectation to the far end of the table where Albert sat, tears streaming down his pale face, shaking his lowered head from side to side while he sobbed and repeated, over and over, "No ...no ...no ...no!"

Finally, Albert rose and wiped the tears from his cheeks. He glanced down the long table at the faces he loved, and then, holding his hands close to his right cheek, he said softly, "No, brother. I cannot go to Nuremberg. It is too late for me. Look what four years in the mines have done to my hands! The bones in every finger have been smashed at least once, and lately I have been suffering

93

from arthritis so badly in my right hand that I cannot even hold a glass to return your toast, much less make delicate lines on parchment or canvas with a pen or a brush. No, brother! For me it is too late."

More than 450 years have passed. By now, Albrecht Durer's hundreds of masterful portraits, pen and silver-point sketches, watercolours, charcoals, woodcuts, and copper engravings hang in every great museum in the world, but the odds are great that you, like most people, are familiar with only one of Albrecht Durer's works. More than merely being familiar with it, you very well may have a reproduction hanging in your home or office.

One day, to pay homage to Albert for all that he had sacrificed, Albrecht Durer painstakingly drew his brother's abused hands with palms together and thin fingers stretched skyward. He called his powerful drawing simply "Hands," but the entire world almost immediately opened their hearts to his great masterpiece and renamed his tribute of love, "**The Praying Hands**."

"Prayer is the opening of the heart to God as to a friend."

"Why should we be reluctant to pray, when Prayer is the Key in the hands of Faith, to open Heaven's Storehouse where are treasured the boundless resources of Omnipotence!" SC 94

The next time you see a copy of that touching creation, take a second look. Let it be your reminder, if you still need one, that no one, **no one - - ever makes it alone!**

THE PRAYING HANDS

Albrecht Durer's Famous Painting.

We too, have a wonderful, loving Brother, Jesus Christ.

In the Book of John chapter 1 and verses 1 and 2, John says;

"In the beginning was the Word, and the Word was with God, and the Word was God. The Same was in the beginning with God. All things were made by Him; and without Him was not anything made that was made."

Then, in verse 14, John also says,

"And the Word was made flesh, and dwelt among us, and we beheld His glory, the glory as of the only begotten of the Father, full of Grace and Truth."

The hands of our brother, Jesus, were stretched out on a wooden cross, and nailed with sharp iron nails piercing His hands and feet, to that cross, by the people He came to save.

As I pointed out earlier, **He was the Omnipotent, Omniscient, Omnipresent, Eternally Existing Creator, Who could have used His Almighty power, and with just one Word, could have wiped out that whole crowd of cruel, hateful people!**

Why didn't He do that? Why didn't the Father who was watching every scene with His heart breaking, speak just one Word and wipe out that crowd of hateful, incredibly cruel crowd of people abusing His only begotten Son?

I'm sure that's what I would have done, and all of you would have done as well, if we had such power in our word!

But because of His **love** for His Creation, and especially for each one of us, who, in the beginning, were made in God's image, He went through such agony and pain of mind, body and spirit, to pay our debt of sin. Let's not forget that everyone of us have transgressed God's Holy Law in some way. **Only Jesus lived a sinless life!**

"For all have sinned and fall short of the glory of God, and all are justified freely by His grace through the redemption that came by Christ Jesus." Romans 3:23-24.

Isaiah 64:6 says, **"All our righteousness is as filthy rags".**

It is gloriously true, that none of God's people, before or after the cross, would be accepted by an immaculately holy God, if the perfect righteousness of Christ were not imputed to us! Because of God's matchless **love**, Christ's righteousness covers us, and we appear in the sight of God as if we had never sinned!

- **"For the wages of sin is death, but the gift of God is eternal life through Jesus Christ our Lord!"** Romans 6:23

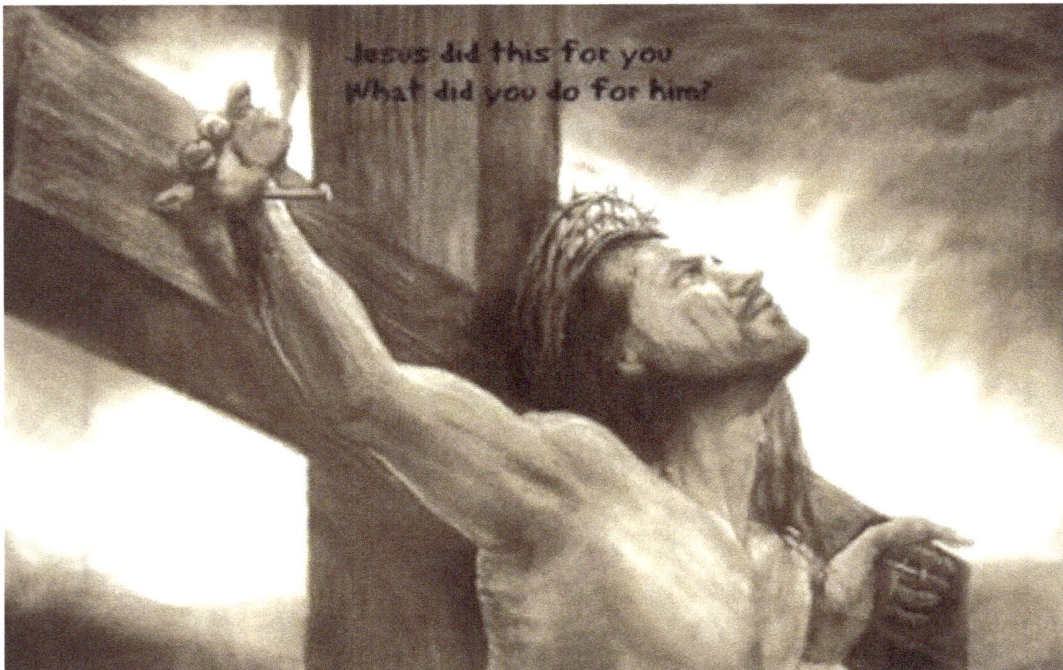

There is no other example known of such incredible LOVE!

CHAPTER 27

PERFECT LOVE CASTS OUT FEAR

1 John 4:18 says very plainly that **"There is no fear in love, for perfect love casts out fear: because fear has torment."**

Most of us have experienced fear at some stage in our lives. Fear can cause so much distress making us very unhappy, preventing us from working, going somewhere, or entering into a relationship with someone.

My daughter suggested I make a list of all that I see as rooted in **LOVE**, with what is the opposite causing **FEAR**. So, I did just that and made two columns, one headed **LOVE** and the other **FEAR**. Here's some of what I listed. No doubt you'll be able to list many more. It was quite a worthwhile exercise. **How thankful are you?**

LOVE	FEAR	LOVE	FEAR
Grateful	Ungrateful	Light	Darkness
Peace	Worry	Fruit	Thorns
Blessings	Curses	Rain in need	Drought
Food	Famine	Clean	Dirty
Health	Sickness	Gladness	Sorrow
Obedience	Disobedience	Salvation	Destruction
Joy	Heartache	Righteousness	Sin
Friends	Enemies	Good	Bad
Singing	Crying	Smiles	Scowls
Trust	Doubt	Life	Death
Happiness	Sadness		
Truth	Lies	*And many, many more.....*	

Where do you and I fit into these lists? How many of the first list, are operating in our lives. How happy, sad or fearful are you and I?

I am quite aware of the fact that sometimes we must face fear and sadness, if we lose someone very dear to us or if we see our friends or loved ones suffering or following wrong paths.

That's when we must cling to the Lord and trust Him as our loving Heavenly Father, come what may, even when nasty experiences happen. A great example of this is the story of Job! After all he suffered at the hands of the enemy of God, he would not give up his trust and faith in God.

Job's determination to trust his Heavenly Father, declaring, **"Though He slay me, yet will I trust Him**!" has always been a wonderful example and inspiration of **LOVE** for me. (Job 13:15)

Another Scripture which gives me inspiration is found in Proverbs 3:5,6.

"Trust in the Lord with all thine heart and lean not on your own understanding. In all your ways acknowledge Him and He shall direct thy paths."

What a loving Father to have as our best Friend, in whom we can place our total faith and trust! We can take all our trials and troubles to Him at any time and know that He loves us dearly, and that **"All things work together for good to them that love Him."** Romans 8:28

To illustrate this truth once more, here's another experience from my own life.

We were home on furlough from New Guinea where my wife and I worked as missionary teachers in the Papuan Gulf, and also in the highlands near Goroka for eleven years. My eldest daughter Caroline, about ten years old at the time, was suffering from tonsilitis, and we left her at Home Hill with my dad and made arrangements with the local doctor to have her tonsils removed on Monday.

We borrowed a friend's car to travel to Brisbane where we had to attend meetings.

The road then between Mackay and Rockhampton was a single lane, and we noticed that there were piles of glass beside the road every few miles and realised that to pass other vehicles on that single lane road, it was necessary to move off the road. Stones would fly up sometimes and smash their windscreens. **So, we stopped and had special prayer for our Heavenly Father to protect our windscreen on our borrowed car.**

It was not even five minutes, before we had to pass another vehicle, and a stone flew up and smashed our windscreen! Hmmm! "Where were you Lord?"

Well, after clearing the glass, we journeyed on, very uncomfortably to Gladstone, and had the windscreen repaired. It was now late Friday afternoon, and we had hoped we wouldn't have to travel on the next day, which was God's special day, the Sabbath. At a petrol station we asked the chap who served us if he knew any Seventh Day Adventists in Gladstone. "Oh yes" he said. "I know the minister, Kevin Moore." He gave us his phone number, and so I called Kevin and explained our predicament, and asked if he could recommend a suitable place for us to stay over the Sabbath.

"No problem, Don! Come and stay with us! It is annual Yacht Race weekend. My wife is playing the piano and I am singing some Gospel songs, so we won't be home. I will give the key to a neighbour for you to go in and make yourselves comfortable. There's food in the fridge, and we should be home round nine o'clock. The address is…"

We had never met these kind people, but sure enough, a neighbour gave us the key and we were able to go in and take a much-needed rest. It was lovely to meet Kevin and his wife when they came home, to thank them for their kindness.

On Sabbath morning we attended the church with the Moores, and after the service, another kind couple invited us to their home for lunch. They had a daughter who had suffered with epilepsy, and despite all the medical treatments, and special prayers, she was still suffering eight or ten serious fits each day.

They told us how they were at wits end to know what to do, when a friend gave them a book called **"Everyone's Guide to Nature Cure" by Harry Benjamin,** and suggested they try using the methods Harry described in his book for this problem. When we visited, their daughter was getting well with only one or two fits a day. They showed us the book, and we were keen to see what it said to do for Tonsilitis. **It described a Juice Fast for at least four days.**

We rang my Dad and told him we were going to try this for Caroline. We also called the doctor and told him to cancel the operation. He was not pleased and told us in plain words what he thought of the plan.

We knew we had a large patch of lovely pineapples at our school in Papua, and so when we returned to our school after furlough, **we tried just pineapple juiced and crushed and other ways, for the four days and indeed the Tonsilitis disappeared!**

Sometime later, when we were transferred to our High School and College at Kabiufa near Goroka, an itinerant nurse visited the staff school and did a health check for the children. She remarked how it seemed Caroline had never had Tonsilitis! We just said, **"Praise the Lord! Thank you so much Heavenly Father for that "little stone" that smashed our windscreen."**

He had a plan that we did not understand at the time it happened. That **"little stone"** started us on a journey of research and study of God's natural ways of healing and caring for our body temples, which we have used and shared with many, many suffering people over the years. **"God is good all the time, and all the time God is good!" What a wonderful loving Father we have!**

It truly is all about LOVE!

CHAPTER 28

WANTED: MEN OF FAITH AND COURAGE

As I mentioned earlier in Chapter 16, **the greatest want of this world is for men of faith and courage:**

"MEN WHO WILL STAND FOR THE RIGHT THOUGH THE HEAVENS FALL".

Again, we have the example of dear **Job**, (see the book by his name in Scripture). In the face of the horrendous attacks of the enemy of God, Lucifer, Job stayed true and faithful to God. His friends deserted him. Even his wife told him to give up and die! Some wife! Then Job's statement of his faith in God, which has always inspired me:

"Though He slay me yet will I trust Him!" (Job 13:15)

Another wonderful man of God, **Abraham**. God told him to take Isaac, his only begotten son, and do as the heathen nations around him, that is, offer Isaac his only son as a sacrifice on Mt Moriah. God had told Abraham earlier that he and Sarah would have a son even though they were both very old, and that Isaac would be the progenitor of a vast nation. Abraham knew God personally and loved Him dearly. He didn't understand why God would ask him to do such a terrible thing to his only son. How could Isaac be the father of many nations, if he killed him?

But he trusted God and was ready to do as He said, when, at the last moment, God shouted out, **"Stop! Do not hurt the boy. Now I know that you really trust Me!".** Then they found a ram caught in a thicket nearby, and offered it instead, as a sacrifice. **Isaac** also trusted his father and was willing to do as God had said. They both loved God and were willing to do as God said, and be obedient to Him, **"though the heavens fall!"** (See the full story in Genesis 22:1-19).

Next, we can consider the example of the three Hebrew boys, **Shadrack, Meshack and Abednego** in the time of Babylon. Nebuchadnezzar had built a great golden image, representing himself as ruler of the world, and commanded that at a certain time, everyone had to bow down and worship the image. Anyone who didn't bow down would be cast into a burning fiery furnace! The boys told Nebuchadnezzar that they would not break God's second commandment and would not bow down and worship anyone but the true God, **"though the heavens fall!:"**

Nebuchadnezzar was very angry and ordered that they be cast into that fiery furnace. Then he saw a fourth person with them who looked like "a son of the gods", as the original text says. When he called them forth, their clothes were not even singed, and not even the smell of smoke was upon them. What a wonderful testimony to all who witnessed the power and love of God for His faithful children. Read the whole incredible story in God's Word. (Daniel chapter 3 verses 1-30.)

Then there is **Noah**. God told him to build a huge ship to be a safe haven for anyone who would trust Him to be saved from a great flood of water, that God was going to send to cleanse the earth of the wickedness that had become so commonplace, much like what is going on in our world today.

Noah told the people what God said was going to happen for <u>one hundred and twenty years</u>. Noah loved and trusted God and built that huge ship, the remains of which have been found on Mt Ararat in Turkey. (See Chapter 3 for the full story of an amateur archaeologist, and other proofs also of God's Word, by Ron Wyatt.)

After all Noah's warnings, the people just laughed and mocked him, and only Noah, his three sons and their wives, and many animals and birds were saved.

Daniel also was a man who loved and trusted God, and even though the king had decreed that anyone who prayed to and worshipped any other god but that of the king, would be cast into a den of lions. Daniel continued at his home, unafraid, with his windows open, to pray to God. His nasty hateful enemies, who had planned it all, reported to the king, that Daniel had not followed his decree.

At evening Daniel was lowered into the den of lions. The king loved Daniel, and in the morning, he hurried to the den and called out, "**Daniel! Has your God been able to protect you from the lions?**" Daniel replied, "**Yes, oh lord!**"

Then the whole plot of Daniel's enemies was made known to the king. He had those wicked hateful men thrown into the den, and the hungry lions quickly had quite a meal of those wicked men! (Daniel chapter 6, verses 10-24.)

What a wonderful witness again, for God's love and care for those who truly love and trust Him!

There are so many more examples, of men and women who had faith and courage, and trusted God, "**though the heavens fall**."

Check God's Word for the stories of Elijah, Joshua, Jeremiah, Moses. Read history at any good Library, for the testimonies of the early Reformers, Wycliffe, Hus, Jerome, Luther, Polycarp, and many more faithful and courageous men and women, who loved and trusted God, and stood faithful to Him "**though the heavens fall**". They were willing to suffer all sorts of terrible persecution to remain faithful to God. Even today, persecution is going on in many communist countries, and other pagan regions, with many, many Christians tortured, threatened and persecuted, and killed for their faith.

These faithful and true men and women of God have always inspired me, and I'd like now to share a couple of personal experiences I've had to face in spite of government edicts, because I too, love God with all my heart, and want to be counted among those who are faithful and true to Him, "**though the heavens fall**".

When I was in my late teens or early twenties, a long time ago, there was threat of another World War, and many Australian young people were conscripted to train as soldiers. Just in case I was commanded to train, I had prepared myself to obey God's law in His Ten Commandments, to not kill anyone, and had determined to save lives instead. Therefore, I trained myself in First Aid, and Home Nursing and obtained certificates in these fields.

Subsequently, I was called up, but I made known to the authorities that I would not train to kill people. I was commanded to face court in Brisbane because of my convictions. I explained why I had chosen to disobey the command of the government but had prepared myself to serve as a Medical Orderly. They could all see that I was not going to go against God's command and had qualified myself in First Aid and Home Nursing. The judge considered my intention to serve my country as a medic and I was acquitted. I had to do three months training at Wacol in Brisbane, and another three months in various locations around Queensland, in the midst of my training as a teacher at Kelvin Grove Teacher's College, but that's another story!

Another example happened in 1983. I was asked to take charge of the Townsville Seventh Day Adventist School. At that time, it was a requirement that all teachers had to be members of the Teacher's Union. I did not intend to join a Union, as I believed it was not according to God's Word to be part of such a worldly group, where I would be required to teach anything they required. We are seeing this demonstrated very clearly at present with teachers in the public schools teaching lots of things contrary to God's specific instructions. Evolution is one thing which is being taught to children and youth.

It was God, who gave the rules in the Ten Commandments, to honour our parents; not to steal; not to tell lies; not to kill; not to commit adultery; not to covet what others have, and to honour and acknowledge their Creator and Redeemer. If we take God "out of the picture", then the Law of the Jungle becomes operative. Isn't this what we are seeing nearly every day on the news? **Young people, even children are stealing cars, smashing property and killing others, to take whatever they wish**. On the news one evening, a policeman apprehending a youngster for breaking and entry and stealing, asked the lad why he did what he did. The boy's answer was simply, **"Because I can!"**.

No God! No laws! Then do whatever you wish!!

Then there is being taught as a requirement now that very young children need a sexual partner! They are taught that they can change sex, masturbate and on and on! Anyone who speaks against such iniquity can be heavily fined or even jailed!

Should those who love and serve God, be punished, and forced to comply with the world's standards? Join a union? No thank you! I had to go to court again in Townsville and explain why I refused to join the Teachers' Union. Fortunately, the judge was a kind man and gave me exemption!

So again, we see the two empires at work more and more, as we near the time when God will say "Enough!" God's empire allows us all to have **free will** to **choose** to **LOVE** Him and keep His laws or **choose** to follow Satan's empire of **FORCE**. We see so many groups today trying to reform the world, and make the politicians and police make people reform, but God's Word says clearly that this is not going to happen. Daniel's book, chapters seven to nine speak of "**a time of trouble coming such as never was since there was a nation"**. In many countries this is already happening. Jesus Himself speaks the same warning in Matthew 24, Mark13, Luke 21 and John in the book of Revelation!

Won't you stop and consider which empire you will **choose, while God's loving offer is still available?** I'm **choosing** my Creator's Kingdom of **LOVE**!

It is truly all about LOVE!

CHAPTER 29

MY EFFORTS TO FULFIL MY DREAM

When I was just a young boy, my father and mother attended a little church group in Townsville. On one particular Sabbath, we had some visitors who were missionaries from the Solomon Islands. They were taking a new mission ship back to the islands and stopped over the Sabbath to worship with us. I was about ten years old and was fascinated to see and hear one of the visitors, whose skin was very black. His name was **Kata Ragoso**. He had fuzzy hair; very white teeth and the whites of his eyes made such a contrast with his black skin. He also was wearing a dress-like thing called a "laplap", and sandals on his feet. He was invited to speak and told us a story that happened during the war.

Kata Ragoso

He told how the Japanese had set up their headquarters in his island and took many islanders to be their slaves to work for them. As Friday arrived Kata Ragoso and a friend with him told the commander that they would not be able to work on Saturday, as it was God's Sabbath. **The commander was very angry and told them that if they would not do as they were told they'd be shot.** Kata told him that they still would not work on the Sabbath, so they were tied up and put in a prison compound with guards in place, to be shot in the morning. They had prayer together and tried to sleep.

During the night a visitor appeared before them, their bonds fell off, and the visitor told them to get up and follow him. He led them past the guards, who never moved, and took them down to the beach where there was a canoe waiting with two paddles in it. The visitor told them to get into the canoe and go home to their village. They did as he said, and turned around to thank him, but there was no one there! **They realized that their visitor was really an angel sent by the Lord, in answer to their prayers and faithful obedience to God's laws!** They went home to their village and were able to avoid being captured again. It reminded me of the story of **Peter** in the Bible! (Acts 12:3-19.)

That story by this black visitor made such an impression on me, just ten years, that right there and there, I decided that my life would be devoted to serving God as a missionary, in the islands of the Pacific Ocean.

I loved building and had majored in Building Construction with timber and metal, trade drawing and perspective at High school, and eventually worked for a year in the cane fields when I finished school, to save enough money to attend Avondale College at Cooranbong, New South Wales, to do the Building Course. My aim was to work as a missionary to build schools and churches for the people of the islands.

The year at Avondale went well till about October, when the accountant called me in and told me that my account was low, and I had not paid for my fees. So, as well as working on the college farm each afternoon, I joined the Sanitarium Health Food factory, also on the college campus, to help make Weetbix. It was a tight routine of classes each morning. Work on the farm each afternoon for four hours. Then a little study till I fell asleep waiting for the alarm to sound at 1.30am to get ready for my shift at the factory at 2am. At 6am I would do swimming from the swing bridge to the point where the creek joined the mainstream, as training for the Life Saving Course I was doing, before changing and rushing up to the dining hall for breakfast, before classes started.

Next to me "on the make", at the factory, was another student, Teddy Rowe, who was twenty-one years old, and I was only seventeen. We were both doing exactly the same job, taking the prepared trays of Weetbix off the trays and loading them onto trolleys to go to the ovens.

Teddy told me he was getting paid seven and six an hour. I was only getting two and six an hour! I was very puzzled by this, and went to the accountant, asking why this was so, when I was doing the very same work. He told me that it was because I was only seventeen and that he was following the government payment schedule. Hmmm!

I struggled on for the rest of the year and had earned just enough to complete all my fees. When I finished the year, the accountant congratulated me and said,

"See you next year Don."

I said, "I don't think so! Bye!"

Well, what was I to do now? I still wanted to work for the Lord. Maybe I should try Colporturing! So, I arranged to board with an old lady in Brisbane. I had a bicycle and planned to try to sell Christian books door to door round Brisbane, but it was rainy season in Queensland in January. Books and rain are not a good combination, and I was again getting further and further behind financially, but I kept trying until about March. I was visiting with some of Ruth's relatives one day, and relating my woes, when the husband, who was a teacher, said,

"Don, why don't you try training as a teacher? Perhaps that's what the Lord wants you to do!"

I had never considered such a life work. I wanted to be a **builder**, and continued to try to do Colporturing till I couldn't even pay my board to the old lady! I had one white terylene shirt, which I washed every evening, and it would be dry in the morning. I was becoming more and more discouraged, to the point that I decided that I would try enrolling as a teacher, as Ruth's cousin had suggested. I took my High School results with me to see the Queensland Government Education minister. I knew the government paid Trainees four pounds ten a week for the first year and five pounds five shillings a week for the second year. **He said it would have been better had I done an Academic Course, instead of Building, but as they were short of teachers, and I had majored in English, he would allow me to try.**

He gave me a letter for the Principal of the Teachers College at Kelvin Grove, who introduced me to a group of about thirty young men also training and I was thrilled to get started. Eventually, a lecturer came in after I'd been there for only a few days or so, with a bundle of envelopes and handed them out to the young men, and there was even one for me. I opened the envelope and was shocked to find nearly one hundred pounds there! I went to the lecturer, and said,

"There is some mistake here sir, as I have only been here a little while".

He said,

"No worries Don! The government always pay new students backpay to January One!"

Can you imagine my surprise and joy? Now I would be able to pay my board owing to the old lady, buy a new shirt and supplies, and other things I desperately needed, and I was "away"! Thank you Lord!

One of the students befriended me, who was a tall Dutch lad whose name was Will Kraa. He was a real friend and was interested in my stand as a Christian. I shared with him my understanding of truth from the Word of God, the Bible. He was very interested and eventually he was baptized, and after teaching awhile, decided to attend Avondale College at Cooranbong in New South Wales, and graduated as a minister of the Gospel. But that's another great story!

I worked as a teacher for the government for seven years, at various locations, even at Home Hill Rural School, where I did my Primary School education. Eventually, the church asked me to be Principal of the **Mona Mona Mission**, an aboriginal school near Kuranda in North Queensland. I had two assistant teachers with me, and we spent two years there teaching the aboriginal children, before the government decided that they wanted to build a dam there and they closed the school and mission station down. Actually, the proposed dam has never been built. Hmmm! **What was I to do now?**

That was when the Church asked me to be a missionary as Principal of a school in the Papuan Gulf in New Guinea. I had married my Ruthie by then and we had three lovely children. We were so thrilled to be able to work as missionaries for the Lord. **My childhood dream was coming true at last!** We had another son and daughter while there in New Guinea in the hot, wet, steamy Gulf for seven years, and then four years in the Highlands at our High School and College near Goroka! But that's another book of stories, in another book I've written, called **"Mission Stories from Home and Abroad."** You can read these stories at my website at www.getwellnstaywell.com , under the heading "**Studies**".

We are often not aware of what God has planned for us, but if we **choose** to devote our lives completely to Him, He has promised to lead and guide us as He sees best. He is a truly loving and wonderful Father, and even though we don't recognize His plans for us, we must realize that if we trust and obey Him, He will provide His plans for us in His timing, not ours!

One of my favourite Scriptures is found in Proverbs 3:5 & 6.

"Trust in the Lord with all thy heart and lean not to thine own understanding. In all thy ways acknowledge Him and He will direct thy paths."

What a wonderful, loving Father we have. If we **choose** to truly love and trust Him, He has promised to direct our paths.

What a loving Creator God!

CHAPTER 30

A FRIEND CLOSER THAN A BROTHER

We all like to have good friends to share our life experiences, to know they are there when and if we need assistance, to share our understandings of truth together and to walk side by side with our Lord. Proverbs 18: 24 says,

"A man that hath friends must shew himself friendly: and there is a Friend that sticks closer than a brother." Proverbs 18:24

Jesus can be our closest and most trustworthy Friend, if we **choose** to love Him, and walk with Him every day, all the way, even when we may not see where He is leading us! He knows what it is like to be one of us, because He **chose** to become one of us by taking on humanity. John 1:1-3 and verse 14.

"In the beginning was the Word, and the Word was with God, and the Word was God.

The same was in the beginning with God.

All things were made by Him; and without Him was not anything made that was made."

"And the Word was made flesh, and dwelt among us, and we beheld His glory, (the glory as of the only begotten of the Father,) full of grace and truth."

Jesus, the Word, the Creator of the universe, took upon Himself, our human nature, by being born of the virgin Mary as a tiny baby boy, as we are born, but with the Holy Spirit as His Father

He had a human nature as well as His Divine Nature! Therefore, He can identify with us. He knows our weaknesses and our griefs. He knows what it is like to be tempted by the Devil, Satan! He showed us how to overcome Satan, by holding fast to God's Word, the Holy Scriptures.

He knows what it is like to be hungry. He knows what it is like to be mocked, rejected and severely and unjustly punished. He knows all too well the pain of body, mind and spirit. He is acquainted with what it is like to have our fallen nature. He knows how to overcome temptation and has demonstrated for us how to live and overcome every defect in our character, just as He overcame and never once did He sin or doubt His Father. He was totally dependent on His Heavenly Father and Their plan to make a way for all His creation to be saved from the penalty of transgression. All that is required of us is to **choose** to accept the wonderful, amazing Gift of our loving God. We have the opportunity to exercise our God-given **freewill** to **choose** to accept or reject His unfathomable **LOVE**!

What a beautiful example of humility and **LOVE**.

In God's Word there are over eighty references to what it is like to have true friends, and also to be mindful that many pretend to be our "friends", while they are simply planning to take advantage of our friendship to gain money, or fame or pleasures!

Judas is a good example, of one who **chose** to be Jesus' friend, while all the while using Jesus' friendship for his own objectives and agenda, to set up the Jewish nation as rulers of the world with wealth and power over all mankind! His motive stemmed from selfishness and pride!

Isn't this what we are seeing today? Mega rich men are planning to rule the world, to set up a New World Order, by forcing all the world to conform to their agenda, to gain even more control, wealth, and power for themselves. In chapter 9, I have already outlined this search for power and control that has been going on for so long.

This motive and selfish desire did not begin here on earth. It began in heaven, when Lucifer tried to make himself the ruler of everything and everyone in the universe. He even convinced one third of the angels to follow him! We can read the rest of this sad story in Genesis and other Scriptures. In Revelation 12: 1-17, you can read the whole sad story:

"And there was war in heaven: Michael, (another name for Jesus, the Word), **and His angels fought against the dragon,** (another name for Lucifer, the devil), **and prevailed not."**

On earth it began in the Garden of Eden. The dragon, in the form of a serpent, convinced Eve to reject God's Word and accept the devils' lies. She convinced Adam to do likewise. Then began the war on earth, which has been going on for almost six thousand years. God had warned Adam and Eve not to disobey His Word or they would die! Cain demonstrated the result of disobedience and tried to take control by killing his brother Abel. Men have been trying to take control of the world ever since, and we are all suffering the result of our first parents' disobedience. All are subject to death right to our day.

But, because God is a God of **LOVE**, and **"is not willing that any should perish"**, (2 Peter 3:9), a plan was already in place, to offer a way for anyone who **chooses** to escape from the penalty of sin, (disobedience to God's Eternal Law of **LOVE**). I have already shared this wonderful plan in preceding chapters. It is all described in the Gospels and is summed up in the most beautiful, and most quoted texts in all God's Word.

John 3:16 and 17. **"For God so <u>loved</u> the world, that he gave His only begotten Son, that whosoever believeth in Him should not perish, but have everlasting life. For God sent not His Son into the world to condemn the world; but that the world through Him might be saved"**.

I can't help feeling emotional every time I think of how loving God is, and what the Father and His Son went through, to offer salvation and eternal life with Him in an earth made new, as He planned for man, made in His image, in the very beginning. **How wonderful to have such a Friend!**

"Thank you! Thank you! Thank you Lord, from the bottom of my heart!"

Jesus as a young boy teaching the elders.

CHAPTER 31

A VERY HELPFUL BOOK OF PRACTICAL ADVICE

God's Word, the Bible, is the most helpful Book of all, for practical living. I have also found another book written by Dale Carnegie, built entirely on God's principles for a very happy, meaningful and successful life.

When Jesus was asked by a lawyer, who was one of the Pharisees, to tell them which was the greatest commandment, He said to,

"Love God first, with all your heart and mind and strength was the greatest commandment, and the second one was like it, to love your neighbour as yourself."

The whole episode is recorded in Matthew's Gospel 22: 35-40

Dale has built his book on these very principles. That's why I have found it very helpful and really abundant in practical advice on how to **"How to Win Friends and Influence People".** It is one of the most popular non-fiction works of our time! I strongly advise everyone to find a copy and read it carefully, putting into practice these very practical ways to make friends, and be able to share the Truths of God's Word with others, and win them to Christ.

I'd like to share some of Dale's advice, with examples, and some from my own experience with you as well. The principles outlined are very significant ways to share the Gospel with everyone you know, with your wife, your children, your relatives and friends and virtually everyone you meet!

He sums up his first chapter with many real-life examples and this good advice to begin with.

 "If you want to gather honey, don't kick over the beehive."

<u>**"In a Nutshell".**</u>

RULE 1. Become genuinely interested in other people. "Love others as yourself." (Matthew 12:31)

RULE 2. Smile. "A merry heart doeth good like a medicine!" (Proverbs 17:22)

An example from my own approach, when I meet people in a store or even on the phone, it always brings a smile to me, and nearly always to the one I am speaking to.

"My name's Don. How are you today?"

Most people often respond with, **"I'm good."**

My answer is, **"Wow! Another good person! I've been trying to be good for over eighty years! How do you do it?"**

That usually brings a smile and we're off to great start.

Sometimes the response is, **"Pretty good."**

"Wow! You are pretty and good as well! That's marvellous! Do you give lessons?"

What a great opportunity, especially if it's a lady or a young girl at the checkout. Definitely a smile appears. Again, you are off to good start once more, to share God's Truth and His love as the opportunity arises.

If it's **"Quite well!"** or **"Very well, thank you!"**

"That's great to hear. It's certainly better than being fat, sick and nearly dead!"

Usually, another smile occurs, and you are off to a good start once more.

RULE 3. Remember that a man's name is the sweetest and most important sound in any language.

Introduce yourself, with, **"My name is Don. What's your name?"**

Usually they will give their name, so address them by their name often.

"Thank you, xxxx. You may be able to tell me ???"

This makes them feel good right away, when speaking directly, or again on the phone, or whatever device you're using. Just recently my wife and I bought a new latest model car, which had so many innovative gadgets and modern additions such as a small camera front and back. Every time we'd start up, a voice said, **"Rear camera disconnected!"**.

After many efforts locally, to have it working we eventually found the phone number for the manufacturer in Melbourne. When I called, he said his name was **Tony**. I introduced myself as **Don,** and asked how he was going, and his reply was,

"I'm good. What can I do for you?"

Aha! After explaining our problem with the rear camera, and our failed efforts to get help locally, I said,

"Tony, how great it is to find a <u>good</u> man at last!" After explaining more of the problem, his response was amazing. He said,

"Don, I think we can help. I'll send you a new rear camera."

I said, **"Tony, That's wonderful of you! I see you are indeed a good man. Thank you so much."**

He said, **"No worries Don, and don't worry about the postage! We'll take care of that."**

Wow! What a great result just by applying the principle in **Rule 3.**

If the person you are speaking to is wearing a name tag, always address them by name, without asking for their name, and they immediately feel great!

RULE 4. Be a good listener.

People are glad if they know you are really listening to what they are sharing.

RULE 5. Talk in terms of the other person's interests.

"I see you love sailing xxx. It's a really lovely yacht you have there. I built my own yacht years ago and love sailing too."

Ask people about their interests and what they value most in life, and they will usually be glad to share, and you have their attention to share experiences."

RULE 6. Make the other person feel important and do it sincerely. "As a man thinketh in his heart, so is he". (Proverbs 23:7)

"You know, I really appreciate how you are so loving and kind and helping so many people who are in need. I wish there were many more people like you!"

Again, I strongly recommend that you seek out a copy of Dale's book, perhaps in your local Library, or online, to become acquainted with simple practical ways to get people's attention and be able to share more efficiently the Gospel message of Salvation as the Lord opens the way.

There are five other chapters in Dale's book which have lots of other helpful, practical, and important principles, and examples, to open the way to share the most important truth of all, God's immeasurable love, and His plan of salvation.

I read a report recently that <u>one in two marriages today,</u> <u>end up in separation or divorce.</u> **That is shocking statistics!** So, here is some more great advice Dale shares for husbands and wives, to save marriages from ending so tragically. He shares ten questions for **Husbands**, and ten questions for **Wives**, taken from a book by Emmet Crozier titled, **"Why Marriages Go Wrong."**

For Husbands:

1. Do you still "court" your wife with an occasional gift of flowers, with remembrance of her birthday and wedding anniversary, or with some unexpected attention, some unexpected tenderness?

2. Are you careful to never criticize her before others?

3. Do you give her money or freedom to spend entirely as she chooses, above the household expenses?

4. Do you make an effort to understand her varying feminine moods, and help her through periods of fatigue, nerves, and irritability?

5. Do you share at least half of your recreation hours with your wife?

6. Do you tactfully refrain from comparing your wife's cooking or housekeeping with that of your mother or of Bill Jones' wife, except to her advantage?

7. Do you take a definite interest in her intellectual life, her clubs and societies, the books she reads, or her views on civic problems?

8. Can you let her receive friendly attentions from other men without making jealous remarks?

9. Do you keep alert for opportunities to praise her, and express your admiration for her?

10. Do you thank her for her little jobs she does for you, such as sewing on a button, darning your socks, or sending your clothes to the dry cleaners?

For Wives:

1. Do you give your husband complete freedom in his business affairs, and do you refrain from criticizing his associates, his choice of a secretary, or the hours he keeps?

2. Do you try your best to make your home interesting and attractive?

3. Do you vary the household menu so that he never knows what to expect when he sits down at the table?

4. Do you have an intelligent grasp of your husband's business, so you can discuss it with him helpfully?

5. Can you meet financial reverses bravely, cheerfully, without criticizing your husband for his mistakes or comparing him unfavourably with other more successful men?

6. Do you make a special effort to get along amiably with his mother or other relatives?

7. Do you dress with an eye for your husband's likes and dislikes in colour and style?

8. Do you compromise little differences of opinion in the interest of harmony?

9. Do you make an effort to learn games or activities your husband enjoys so you can share his leisure hours?

10. Do you keep track of the day's news, the new books, and new ideas, so you can hold your husband's interest?

If you are having marital problems, do check out these great ideas to turn your marriage around, and enjoy continued happiness together.

There is so much more in Dale's book that is really good practical advice for all those who love God and want to effectively share Hs amazing LOVE.

In Matthew 22:36-40 Jesus emphasizes how important is love for others. Trying to corner Jesus, the Pharisees asked,

"Master, which is the greatest commandment in the law?

Jesus replied, _Thou shalt love the Lord thy God with all thy heart, and with all thy soul, and with all thy mind._ This is the first and greatest commandment. And the second is like unto it, _Thou shalt love thy neighbour as thyself._ On these two commandments, hang all the law and the prophets."

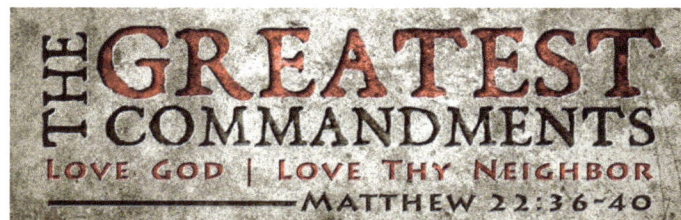

Again, it's all about LOVE!

CHAPTER 32

THE TIME OF THE END

In this chapter I'd like to review the most amazing and very important subject of all for God's true people, as we face the climax and closing of this world as we know it, and what is soon to occur according to God's Word. In Daniel's Old Testament Book, Chapter 12 and verse 1, it says,

"And at that time, (the time of the end), **shall Michael,** (another name for Jesus), **stand up, the great prince which standeth for the children of thy people;** _and there shall be a time of trouble such as never was since there was a nation_ **even to that same time: and at that time thy people shall be delivered, everyone that shall be found written in the book."**

In the New Testament book of Matthew chapter 24 and verse 21, Jesus Himself says in almost identical words to Daniel's statement,

**"For then shall be great tribulation such as was not since the beginning of this world to this time, no, nor ever shall be."**

Matthew 24: 15, Jesus also says,

"When ye shall therefore see the abomination of desolation, _spoken of by Daniel the prophet,_ **stand in the Holy Place…"**

Jesus is saying clearly, to go and study Daniel the prophet! This was just one of Jesus' signs He gave to His disciples, in answer to their question in Matthew 24: 3,

"What shall be the sign of thy coming, and of the end of the world?"

Surely, we are nearing this time now, when we see all the signs fulfilling rapidly just as Jesus gave us, _just in our lifetimes!_

In Chapter 12, I have dealt in detail with the signs we are seeing now, fulfilling and increasing in intensity, as we come to the climax of this world of sin, suffering and death.

Before going further, I need to deal with a very common belief that a day in prophecy is really a year.

The texts that many people use, are found in **Numbers 14:34,** and **Ezekiel 4: 6.** When we examine both these texts, we find that in **Numbers** the Lord allotted the Israelites, forty years of exile wandering in the desert till all the adults had died. This was the allotted **punishment** God served upon them because they believed the ten spies, **rather than trusting the Lord to care for them, as Joshua and Caleb encouraged them to do, to believe God's promises and trust Him.**

This definitely had nothing to do with prophecy in any way. **To use this text to apply to prophecy is lifting the text out of <u>context</u>, which then becomes a <u>pretext,</u> giving an entirely misuse of Scripture, to suit man's understanding of God's Word.**

In **Ezekiel**, the Lord told him to lie on his side for forty days to show how long the Israelites would suffer punishment, for their years of distrusting their Heavenly Father. Those forty days lying on his side would show a day for a year of punishment they would have to endure for disbelieving and distrusting God.

This example is actually the opposite of what God said in Numbers, and again has nothing to do with prophecy, and especially nothing to do with Daniel's prophecies. In Numbers God gave them **forty years** punishment, for **forty days** of disbelief, and in Ezekiel God told Ezekiel to lie on his side **for forty days to show the years of unbelief of the Jewish people,** to the time of the destruction of Jerusalem.

Daniel's prophecies in Chapters 7 to 12, are all about **"the time of the end"**, which **Daniel mentions about ten times in these chapters**.

In Daniel Chapter 4 we read an amazing story of proud king Nebuchadnezzar, and a dream that he saw, and how Daniel explained to him what God said was going to happen to him, because of his pride and sinful ways!

He would become changed and eat grass like the animals *for seven times*!

Now if those *seven times,* were really years, then we need to multiply 360 days for a Jewish Year by seven. By applying the **"day for a year theory"**, then the king would be eating grass for 2,520 years, which is absurd!

There is a very well-founded law of Bible Study, the **law of *Precedence,* or *First Usage!*** In other words, when a word like **times** is used as in Nebuchadnezzar's dream and in Daniel's explanation, **seven times** could only mean **seven literal years**.

So, when in the same book, Daniel 7: 25, Daniel speaks of a **time, times and a dividing of time.** Surely, we must honestly accept that the **time, times and dividing of time** must be **three and a half *literal* years!** (One year, two years and six months.)

Some Bible scholars take the **two thousand three hundred *days*** as in Daniel Chapter 8: 14, to mean **two thousand three hundred *years,*** when in the same book and same chapter in verse 26, Daniel, speaking of the very same vision the Lord gave him, calls the time in this vision, **two thousand three hundred *evenings and mornings.*** *"days"* is a supplied word by the translators, in Verse 14 and is given in answer to a question asked by two saints Daniel saw in his vision.

"How long will be the vision concerning the daily sacrifice, and the transgression of desolation, to give both the sanctuary and the host to be trodden underfoot." Daniel 8:13

Verse 14 is the answer to this question. Two thousand three hundred evening sacrifices and two thousand three hundred morning sacrifices, making a **literal** twenty-four hours or one day…two sacrifices each day, which means **eleven hundred and fifty literal days,** which fit within the **literal "time, times and a dividing of time", 42 months, and 1260 days or a literal three and a half years!**

This then is a fulfilment of Daniel's **"time of trouble such as never was,"** at the **"time of the end"** in Daniel's chapters 7-12.

Jesus' words in Matthew 24 say plainly that **"unless those days, (of the time of trouble), be shortened, there would be no flesh saved."**

1150 days is a shortening of the <u>literal</u> "time, times and dividing of time," a <u>literal</u> three and a half years, and also the <u>literal</u> 1260 days and the literal 42 months that John speaks about in the Revelation.

In Revelation chapters 11 to 13, John speaks about this time of trouble in detail. If we take John's 1260 days and his 42 months to mean years, we lose the meaning entirely of this important portrayal of what is soon to break upon this world as an over-whelming surprise!

These graphic prophetic portrayals of what is ahead for us who are at the **"time of the end"**, are desperately needed warnings for all people, to see that **"there is a cliff edge ahead"**, (Chapter 10). This whole demonstration of God's love will soon end. The **"the door of the ark will soon be shut"**, (as in the time of Noah). **The time of God's grace will soon end. The time of probation will soon close.**

Only those who have **chosen** to accept God's loving offer of life eternal in a recreated world without end, (Daniel 2), will be saved! Only those, who from the time of Adam and Eve, who have **chosen** to accept Jesus Christ, their promised Deliverer, will have their names written in the Lamb's Book of Life, and will enjoy eternity with our loving God in an earth made new!

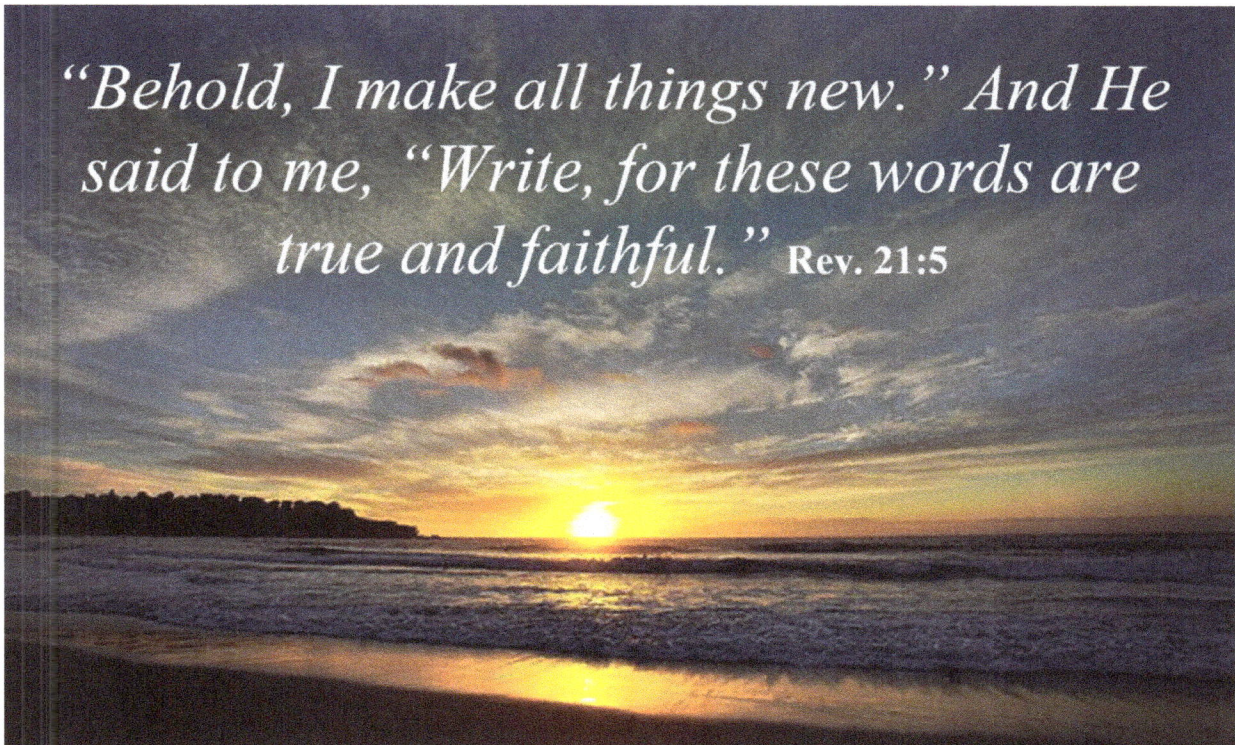

"Behold, I make all things new." And He said to me, "Write, for these words are true and faithful." Rev. 21:5

Once more it is all about LOVE.

CHAPTER 33

REMEMBER

One of the greatest truths found in the Scriptures, misunderstood by so many today, even by most of the Protestant Churches, is found in the Ten Commandments. This is the only part of God's Book, the Bible, that God Himself wrote on two stone tablets, using His own fiery finger, **TWICE**! These two stone tablets God handed to Moses on Mt Sinai. How important then is this passage of Scripture in all the Bible! You'll find all the details of how this came about in the Book of Exodus, Chapters 19 & 20, and 32 to 34.

In the very heart of the Ten Commandments, is a _special command which identifies Who God is._ It begins with _"REMEMBER."_.

Below is this very important fourth commandment as it is written in God's Word. It begins in Exodus 20:8 and completes in verse 11.

"Remember the Sabbath day to keep it holy.

Six days shalt thou labour, and do all thy work:

But the seventh day is the Sabbath of the LORD thy God: in it thou shalt not do any work, thou nor thy son, nor thy daughter, thy manservant, nor thy maidservant, nor thy cattle, nor thy stranger that is within thy gates:

For in six days the LORD made heaven and earth, the sea, and all that in them is, and rested the seventh day: wherefore the LORD blessed the seventh day and hallowed it."

What is the seventh day of the week? Until just recently, the **SEVENTH DAY** has always been what we call **SATURDAY**, but now it is hard to find any diary or calendar that starts on **SUNDAY the first day of the week.** They now are starting on **MONDAY** as the first day of the week, which now makes the **SEVENTH DAY SUNDAY**! How cunning is the great deceiver, Satan.

Most of the Protestant churches are hallowing **SUNDAY** as the holy day to worship God, on the false Sabbath, unaware that they are worshipping on the day that Satan has arranged to replace the true Sabbath Day.

Why do Christians consider the rest of the commandments very important and teach them as the way we should live, but discard the most important commandment identifying Who God is? They teach and believe that:

we should have no other gods before the LORD!

we should not make any images or bow down to them!

we should never use God's name in vain!

We should always honour our father and mother!

We should not kill.

We should not commit adultery.

We should not steal.

We should not tell lies.

We should not covet what others have.

So, why do the majority of Christians discard the **fourth commandment**, which is key to identifying Who God is? He is the eternal Creator of the universe. He never began but has ever existed! That is truly beyond my simple understanding, one who is just one of his created beings!

He is so **omnipotent!** My small mind cannot comprehend such power!

"He just speaks, and it is done. He commands and it stands fast!" Psalms 33:9.

He is **omniscient!** He knows everything! He can even tell exactly what is going to happen in the future **BEFORE** it happens! Again, I cannot imagine such ability! That is way beyond me! We think Google is very clever and knows everything but doesn't come anywhere close to our omniscient Creator.

"Declaring the end from the beginning, and from ancient times the things that are not yet done." Isaiah 46:10

"For there is not a word in my tongue, but You, O Lord, knoweth it altogether!" Psalms 139: 4

He is **omnipresent!** Wow! He can be everywhere at once! He can see everything that is happening in the whole world! He can hear and answer my brother's prayers in England, and my prayers here in Australia, at the same time. He can hear and answer the prayers of every person everywhere, at the same time! Again, that is way beyond my ability to understand. We have wonderful technology such as Zoom today, but it doesn't come close to our Heavenly Father's "Zoom."

Shouldn't we **Remember**, celebrate, and worship such an amazing Being, on the very special day, the seventh day of the week, the Sabbath, that He put in place when He finished His work of Creation?

"Remember the Sabbath day to keep it holy. Six days shalt thou do all thy work but the _seventh_ day is the Sabbath of the Lord thy God…. wherefore the Lord blessed the Sabbath and hallowed it."

See Exodus 20: verses 8 to 11 again, for the full text about God's Sabbath, and why He has commanded us to **REMEMBER** His special day.

The great deceiver the Devil, Satan, has supplanted Sunday as the sabbath day of his empire, and so many Christians are blindly following the customs of men, without being aware of the deceitfulness of the enemy of God! There is not one word of Scripture to support the change of the Sabbath to Sunday, the first day of the week.

So many faithful, loving Christian people, who really love God with all their hearts, are unknowingly worshipping the Lord on the day that the great Deceiver has put in place of the fourth commandment, which identifies our loving Creator. God says the seventh day is His special holy day, not the first day! For thousands of years, the seventh day of the week has always been Saturday as we call it, NOT Sunday!

We remember birthdays and anniversaries of our loved ones because we love them. Shouldn't we REMEMBER the special weekly anniversary of the work of our incredibly loving, wonderful Creator God? I want to show Him I truly love Him by keeping His special seventh day holy to REMEMBER His love for me! Won't you join me?

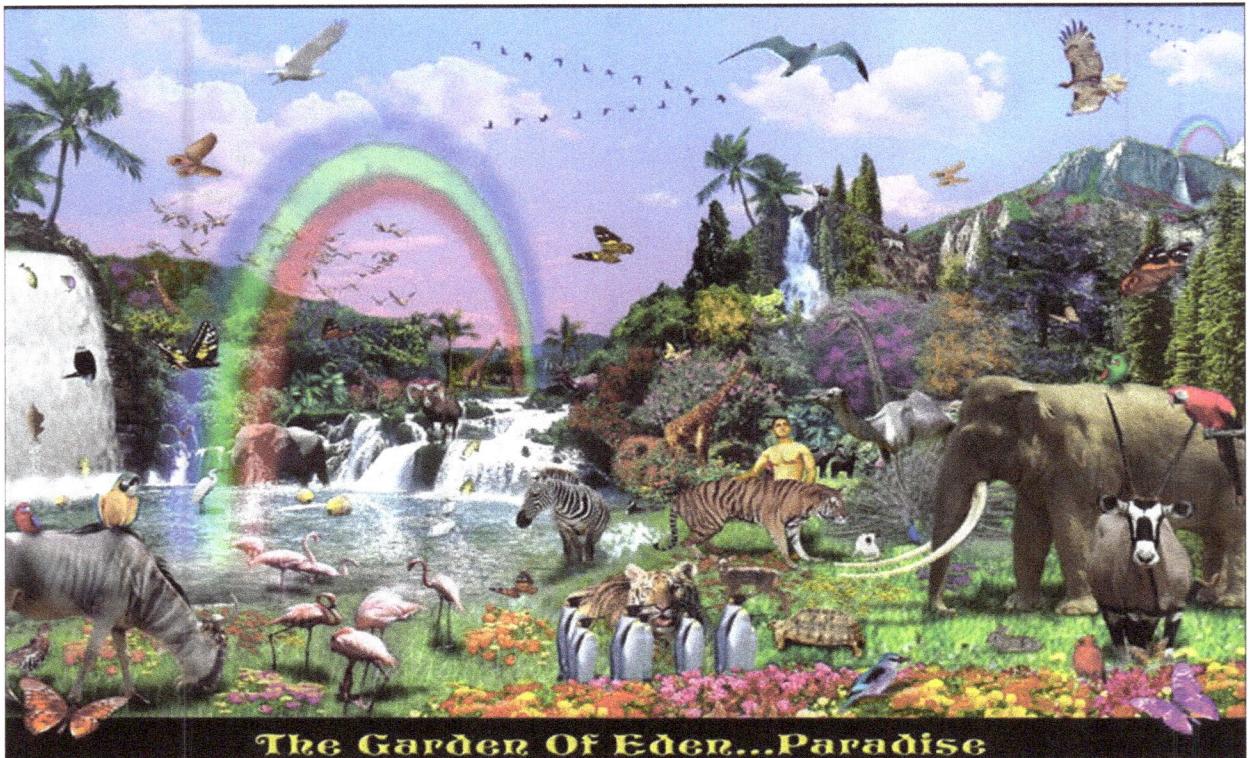

What a world of LOVE our Creator made!

CHAPTER 34

ROME'S CHALLENGE TO PROTESTANTISM

In this chapter I will share some startling challenges from the church of Rome, for which we have no Scriptural answers! I have a very interesting little booklet from which I'd like to share some short extracts with you. The booklet is called,

"ROME'S CHALLENGE. Why Do Protestants Keep Sunday? Taken from the *Catholic Mirror."*

The *Catholic Mirror* was the official organ of Cardinal Gibbons and the Papacy in the United States. There were four editorials printed in 1893, on September 2, 9, 16 and 23. The first statement by the Roman church about their church is headed,

THE CHRISTIAN SABBATH   (All bolding is mine for emphasis.)

(From the *Catholic Mirror* of September 2, 1893)

"Our attention has been called to the above subject in the past week, (The Christian Sabbath"), by the receipt of a brochure of twenty-one pages, published by the International Religious Liberty Association, entitled, "Appeal and Remonstrance", embodying resolutions by the General Conference of the Seventh Day Adventists (Feb 24,1893). The resolutions criticize and censure, with much acerbity, the action of the United States Congress, and of the Supreme Court, for invading the rights of the people by closing the World's Fair on Sunday.

The Adventists are the only body of Christians with the Bible as their teacher, who can find no warrant in its pages for the change of day from the seventh day to the first. Hence their appellation, "Seventh Day Adventists". Their cardinal principle consists of setting apart Saturday for the exclusive worship of God, in conformity with positive command of God Himself, repeatedly reiterated in the sacred books of the Old and New Testaments, literally obeyed by the children of Israel for thousands of years to this day and endorsed by the teaching and practice of the Son of God whilst on earth.

Per contra, the Protestants of the world, the Adventists excepted, with the *same* Bible as their cherished and sole infallible teacher, by their practice, since their appearance, in the sixteenth century, with the time-honoured practice of the Jewish people before their eyes, have rejected the day named for his worship, and assumed, in apparent contradiction of His command, a day for his worship, never once referred for that purpose, in the pages of that Sacred Volume…..

The Protestant world has been, from its infancy, in the sixteenth century, in thorough accord with the Catholic Church, in keeping "holy", not Saturday, but Sunday…..

It resolves itself into a few plain questions easy of resolution:

1st, Which day of the week does the Bible enjoin to be kept holy?

2nd, Has the New Testament modified by precept or practice the original command?

3rd, Have Protestants, since the sixteenth century, obeyed the command of God by keeping "holy" the day enjoined by their infallible teacher, the Bible? and if not, why not?

To the above three questions we pledge ourselves to furnish as many intelligent answers, which cannot fail to vindicate the truth and uphold the deformity of error.

(From the *Catholic Mirror* of SEPT.9, 1893.)

"But faith, fanatic faith, once wedded fast

To some dear falsehood, hugs it to the last."

Moore.

Conformably to our promise in our last issue, we proceed to unmask one of the most flagrant errors and most unpardonable inconsistencies of the Biblical rule of faith. Lest, however, we be misunderstood, we deem it necessary to premise that **Protestantism recognizes no rule of faith, no teacher, save the "infallible Bible". As the Catholic yields his judgement in spiritual matters implicitly, and with unreserved confidence, to the voice of his church, so, too, the Protestant recognizes *no teacher but the Bible.*** All his spirituality is derived from its teachings. It is to him the voice of God addressing him through his sole inspired teacher. It embodies his religion, his faith, and his practice. The language of Chillingworth. "The Bible, the whole Bible, and nothing but the Bible, is the religion of Protestants," is only one form of the same idea multifariously converted into other forms, such as "the Book of God", "The Charter of our Salvation", "the Oracle of Our Christian Faith", "God's Textbook of the Race of Mankind", etc, etc. It is then, an incontrovertible fact that the *Bible alone* is the teacher of Protestant Christianity. Assuming this fact, we will now proceed to discuss the merits of the question involved in our last issue.

Recognizing what is undeniable, the fact of a direct contradiction between the teaching of Protestant Christianity—the Seventh Day Adventists excepted--- on the one hand, and that of the Jewish people on the other, both observing different days of the week for the worship of God, we will proceed to take the testimony of the only available witness in the premises: viz., the teacher common to both claimants, the Bible…..

In the Old Testament, reference is made one hundred and twenty-six times to the Sabbath, and all these texts conspire harmoniously in voicing the will of God commanding the seventh day to be kept, because God Himself *first kept it,* making it obligatory on all as *"a perpetual covenant."…..*

We deem it necessary to be perfectly clear on this point, for reasons that will appear more fully hereafter. The Bible – the Old Testament – confirmed by the living tradition of a weekly practice for 3383 years by the chosen people of God, teaches, then, with absolute certainty, that God, Himself, named the day to be "kept holy to Him." – that the day was Saturday, and that any violation of that command was punishable with death. "Keep you My Sabbath, for it is holy unto you; he that shall profane it shall be put to death; he that shall do any work in it, his soul shall perish in the midst of his people." Ex. 31:14…..

Examining the New Testament from cover to cover, critically, we find the Sabbath referred to sixty-one times. We find, too, that the Saviour invariably selected the Sabbath (Saturday) to

teach in the synagogues and work miracles. The four Gospels refer to the Sabbath (Saturday) fifty-one times.

In one instance the Redeemer refers to Himself as "the Lord of the Sabbath," as mentioned by Matthew and Luke, but during the whole record of His life, whilst invariably keeping and utilizing the day (Saturday), He never once hinted at a desire to change it. His apostles and personal friends afford to us a striking instance of their scrupulous observance of it *after His death*, and whilst His body was yet in the tomb, Luke (23:56) informs us: "And they returned and prepared spices and ointments, and rested on the Sabbath day according to the commandment."…..

Can anything, therefore, be more conclusive than that the apostles and the holy women never knew any Sabbath but Saturday, up to the day of Christ's death?.....

Nine times **do we find the Sabbath referred to in the Acts, but it is the Saturday (the old Sabbath). Should our readers desire the proof, we refer them to chapter and verse in each instance. Acts 13:14, 27,42, 44. Once more, Acts 15:21; again, Acts 16:13; 17:2; 18:4. "And he (Paul) reasoned in the synagogue every Sabbath, and persuaded the Jews and the Greeks." Thus the Sabbath (Saturday) from Genesis to Revelation!!!.....**

Hence the conclusion is inevitable; viz., that of those who follow the Bible as their guide, the Israelites and Seventh-day Adventists have the exclusive weight of evidence on their side, whilst the biblical Protestant has not a word in self-defence for his substitution of Sunday for Saturday. More anon.

(From the *Catholic Mirror* of Sept.16, 1893)

When his satanic majesty, who was "a murderer from the beginning," "and the father of lies," undertook to open the eyes of our first mother, Eve, by stimulating her ambition, " You shall be as gods, knowing good and evil," his action was but the first of many plausible and successful efforts employed later, in the seduction of millions of her children. Like Eve, they learn too late, alas! the value of the inducements held out to allure her weak children from allegiance to God…..

Having proved to a demonstration that the Redeemer, *in no instance*, had, during the period of His life, deviated from the faithful observance of the Sabbath (Saturday), referred to by the four evangelists fifty-one times, although He had designated Himself "Lord of the Sabbath," He never having once, by command or practice hinted at a desire on His part to change the day by the substitution of another and having called special attention to the conduct of the apostles and the holy women, the very evening of His death, securing beforehand spices and ointments to be used in embalming His body the morning after the Sabbath (Saturday), as St Luke so clearly informs (Luke 24:1), thereby placing beyond peradventure, the divine action and will of the Son of God during life by keeping the Sabbath steadfastly; and having called attention to the action of His living representatives after His death, as proved by St Luke; having also placed before our readers *the indisputable fact* **that the apostles for the following thirty years** *(Acts)* **never deviated from the practice of their divine Master in this particular, as St. Luke (Acts 18:4) assures us: "And he (Paul) reasoned in the synagogues** *every Sabbath* **(Saturday), and persuaded the Jews and the Greeks**".....

The first reference to Sunday after the resurrection of Christ is to be found in St Luke's Gospel, chapter 24, verses 33-40, and St John 20:19.

The above texts themselves refer to the sole motive of this gathering on the part of the apostles. It took place on the day of the resurrection (Easter Sunday), not for the purpose of inaugurating "the new departure" from the old Sabbath (Saturday) by keeping "holy" the new day, for there is not a hint given of prayer, exhortation, or the reading of the Scriptures, but it indicates the utter demoralization of the apostles by informing mankind that **they were huddled together in that room in Jerusalem *"for fear of the Jews,"* as St John, quoted above, plainly informs us**.

The second reference to Sunday is to be found in St John's Gospel, 20th chapter, 26th to 29th verses: "And after eight days, the disciples were again within, and Thomas with them." The resurrected Redeemer availed Himself of this meeting of all the apostles to confound the incredulity of Thomas, who had been absent from the gathering on Easter Sunday evening. This would have furnished a golden opportunity to the Redeemer to change the day in the presence of all His apostles, but we state the simple fact that, on this occasion, as on Easter day not a word is said of prayer, praise, or reading of the Scriptures.

The third instance on record, wherein the apostles were assembled on Sunday, is to be found in Acts 2:1: "The apostles were all of one accord in one place." (Feast of Pentecost – Sunday.) Now, will this text afford to our Biblical Christian brethren a vestige of hope that Sunday substitutes, at length, Saturday? For when we inform them that the Jews had been keeping *this Sunday* for 1500 years and have been keeping it for eighteen centuries after the establishment of Christianity, at the same time keeping the weekly Sabbath, there is not to be found either consolation or comfort in this text. Pentecost is the fiftieth day after the Passover, which was called the Sabbath of weeks, consisting of seven times seven days; and the day after the completion of the seventh weekly Sabbath day, was the chief day of the entire festival, necessarily Sunday. What Israelite would not pity the cause that would seek to discover the origin of the keeping of the first day of the week in his festival of Pentecost, that has been kept by him yearly for 3,000 years? Who but the Biblical Christian, driven to the wall for a pretext to excuse his sacrilegious desecration of the Sabbath, always kept by Christ and His apostles, would have resorted to the Jewish festival of Pentecost for his act of rebellion against his God and his teacher, the Bible?.....

"And upon the first day of the week, when the disciples came together to break bread," etc.....

Acts 2:46: "And they, continuing *daily* in the temple, and breaking bread from house to house," etc. Who does not see at a glance that the text produced to prove the exclusive prerogative of Sunday, vanishes into thin air – an *ignis fatuus* – when placed in juxtaposition with the 46th verse of the same chapter? What the Biblical Christian claims by this text for *Sunday alone* the same authority, St. Luke, informs us was *common to every day of the week:*

"And they, continuing *daily* in the temple, and breaking bread from house to house."

One text more presents itself, apparently leaning toward a substitution of Sunday for Saturday. It is taken from St. Paul, 1 Cor. 16:1,3: "Now concerning the collection for the saints, "On the first day of the week, let every one of you lay by him in store," etc. Presuming that the request of St. Paul had been strictly attended to, let us call attention to what had been done each Saturday during the Saviour's life and continued for thirty years after, as the book of Acts informs us.

The followers of the Master met *"every Sabbath"* to hear the word of God; the Scriptures were read *"every Sabbath day."* "And Paul, as his manner was to reason in the synagogue *every Sabbath,* interposing the name of the Lord Jesus," etc. Acts 18:4. What more absurd conclusion than to infer that reading of the Scriptures, prayer, exhortation, and preaching, *which formed the routine duties of every Saturday*, as has been abundantly proved, were overslaughed by a request to take up a collection on another day of the week?.....

Having disposed of every text to be found in the New Testament referring to the Sabbath (Saturday), and to the first day of the week (Sunday); and having shown conclusively from these texts, that, so far, not a shadow of pretext can be found in the Sacred Volume for the Biblical substitution of Sunday for Saturday; it only remains for us to investigate the meaning of the expressions "Lord's Day," and "day of the Lord," to be found in the New Testament, which we propose to do in our next article, and conclude with apposite remarks on the incongruities of a system of religion which we shall have proved to be indefensible, self-contradictory, and suicidal......

Rome's Challenge

Official Catholic quotes regarding
"Sunday Observance"

CHAPTER 35

ROME'S CHALLENGE CONTINUES

(From the *Catholic Mirror* of Sept. 23, 1893)

> **"Halting on crutches of unequal size.**
>
> **One leg by truth supported,** *one by lies.*
>
> **Thus sidle to the goal with awkward pace,**
>
> **Secure of nothing but to lose the race."**

In the present article we propose to investigate carefully a new (and the last) class of proof assumed to convince the Biblical Christian that God had substituted Sunday for Saturday for His worship in the new law, and that the divine will is to be found recorded by the Holy Ghost in apostolic writings.....

The first text of this class is to be found in the **Acts of the Apostles 2:20. "The sun shall be turned into darkness, and the moon into blood, before that great and notable** *day of the Lord shall come."* How many Sundays have rolled by since that prophecy was spoken? So much for that effort to pervert the meaning of the sacred text from the judgment day to Sunday!

The second text of this class is to be found in **1 Cor. 1:8: "Who shall also confirm you unto the end, that you may be blameless** *in the day of our Lord Jesus Christ."* What simpleton does not see that the apostle here plainly indicates the day of judgment? The next text of this class that presents itself is to be found in the same **Epistle, chapter 5:5: "To deliver such a one to Satan for the destruction of the flesh, that the spirit may be saved** *in the day of the Lord Jesus."*

Sunday, or the day of judgment, which? The fifth text is **from St. Paul to the Philippians, chapter 1, verse 6: "Being confident of this very thing, that He who hath begun a good work in you will perfect it** *until the day of Jesus Christ."* The good people of Philippi, in attaining perfection on the following Sunday, could afford to laugh at our modern rapid transit!

We beg leave to submit our sixth of the class; viz., **Philippians, first chapter tenth verse: "That he may be sincere without offense unto** *the day of Christ."* That day was next Sunday, forsooth! Not so long to wait after all. The seventh text, **2 Peter 3:10:** *"But the day of the Lord will come* **as a thief in the night."** The application of this text to Sunday passes the bounds of absurdity.

The eighth text, **2 Peter 3:12: "Waiting for and hastening** *unto the coming of the day of the Lord,* **by which the heavens being on fire, shall be dissolved"** etc. This day of the Lord is the same referred to in the previous text, the application of both of which *to Sunday next* would have left the Christian world sleepless the Saturday night.....

The nineth text wherein we meet the expression "the Lord's day," is the last to be found in the apostolic writings. The Apocalypse, or Revelation, chapter 1:10, furnishes it in the following words of St John: "I was in the Spirit on the Lord's day;" but it will afford no more comfort to our Biblical friends than its predecessors of the same series. Has St. John used the expression previously in his Gospel or Epistles? – Emphatically, *No*. Has he had occasion to refer to Sunday hitherto? – Yes, twice. How did he designate Sunday on these occasions? Easter Sunday was called by (John 20:1) *"The first day of the week."* Evidently, although inspired, both in his Gospel and Epistles, he called Sunday "the first day of the week." On what grounds, then, can it be assumed that he dropped that designation? Was he *more inspired* when he wrote the Apocalypse, or did he adopt a new title for Sunday, because it was now in vogue?.....

We have studiously and accurately collected from the New Testament every available proof that could be adduced in favour of a law cancelling the Sabbath day of the old law, or one substituting another day for the Christian dispensation.....

The Christian Sabbath is therefore to this day, the acknowledged off-spring of the Catholic Church as spouse of the Holy Ghost, without a word of remonstrance from the Protestant world.....

Nor are the limits of demoralization yet reached. Far from it. *Their pretence* for leaving the bosom of the Catholic Church was for apostasy from the truth as taught in the written word. They adopted the written word as their sole teacher, which they had no sooner done than they abandoned it promptly, as these articles have abundantly proved; and by a perversity as wilful as erroneous, they accept the teaching of the Catholic Church in direct opposition to the plain, unvaried and constant teaching of their sole teacher in the most essential doctrine of their religion, thereby emphasizing the situation in what may be aptly designated "a mockery, a delusion and a snare."

Our loving Heavenly Father has specified very clearly in His Holy Word, that He is our loving Creator and Redeemer, Who set up the **Sabbath, the seventh day of the week, (Saturday as we know it today), as the day He has specified as His Holy Day.**

The majority of the Protestant churches, in keeping Sunday, (the first day of the week), as God's Sabbath, are simply following the Papacy, the Roman Catholic Church, from which they broke away, *protesting* and *claiming* that they are following the Word of God, when in reality they are still following the edicts and changes made by the Papacy to God's Holy and immutable, unchangeable law.

How deceitful is the enemy of God! He has even arranged for most of the modern calendars and diaries to start the week on Monday as the first day of the week, **making the seventh day of the week Sunday.** This is just another one of Satan's subtle tactical lies cunningly implanted to deceive men into following him, instead of obeying the command of our loving Heavenly Father!

Why am I emphasizing all this about the true Sabbath of the Lord?

I believe it is to be one of the most important deciding factors in determining who have <u>chosen</u> to accept God's gracious offer of salvation and be part of His Kingdom of LOVE.

The Scriptures show this clearly from the pen of the apostle John in the book of Revelation, chapter 14: 6-12.

The messages of these three angels, are the final warning message to "every nation, kindred, tongue and people"! We all must be ready to **choose** whether we are to be part of Satan's Kingdom, Babylon, or part of our loving Heavenly Father's Kingdom. God's people are those who **choose** "to stand for the right though the heavens fall", and who **choose** to follow God. They are described clearly in verse 12, which says:

"Here is the patience of the saints: <u>here are they that keep the commandments of God,</u> and the faith of Jesus."

Jesus also says plainly, "If you love me, keep My commandments"! John14:15

We don't keep His commandments and counsels to earn salvation. We cannot, of ourselves, earn salvation, by trying to be "good", and going to church regularly, or striving to keep His commandments. We keep His Commandments because of His unfathomable LOVE for all mankind.

When we truly love God, we will keep His Ten Commandments, **"for His commands are not grievous." I John 5:3**

1. *We* would never have anyone else in His place!

2. *We* would never make idols of wood or stone in God's place!

3. *We* would never use His name irreverently!

4. *We* would never forget our Creator on His seventh-day Sabbath!

5. *We* would always honour our parents!

6. *We* would never kill people!

7. *We* would never engage in adultery!

8. *We* would never steal!

9. *We* would never tell lies!

10. *We* would not long for someone else's possessions!

How did these ten laws of life come about? God's Word says God actually wrote them on two tables of stone with His own fiery finger, twice, as I've shown in earlier chapters.

If we teach our children and young people that everything just evolved somehow after a "Big Bang" happened billions of years ago, and that their ancestors evolved from something that slithered out of a swamp perhaps, then they do not need to keep any laws. The laws of the jungle, **"survival of the fittest"**, are the only laws they need to live by, and isn't this what we are seeing happening everywhere today. The news every day now is full of crime especially among young people.

When we take God out of the equation, the laws He put in place become extinct. Building bigger Detention Centres and employing more and more Police is not the way this problem can be fixed. The Word of God shows clearly how this can be accomplished.

Won't you join with me in exercising your gift of FREEWILL, <u>choosing</u> to accept His loving proposal; <u>choosing</u> to keep His Ten Commandments and be part of His Family and His everlasting kingdom of LOVE, because we love Him so? He is LOVE personified! I John 4:8

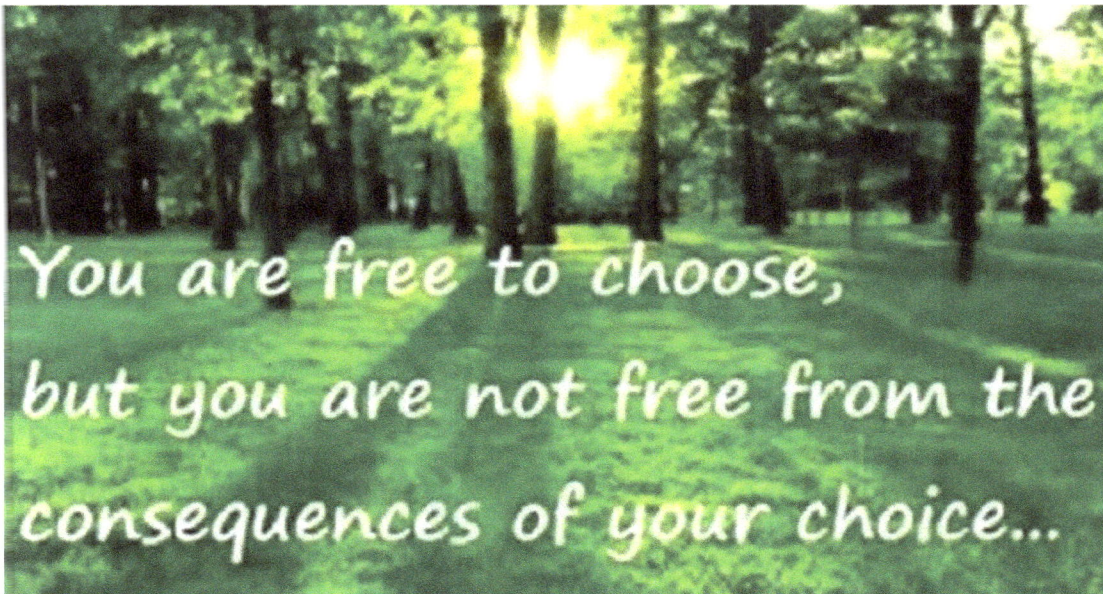

I'm <u>choosing</u> His Kingdom of LOVE!

CHAPTER 36

IMPORTANT TRUTHS FOR OUR GENERATION

As we see events and signs that tell us we are in what Daniel and Jesus called the **"time of the end"**, we need to be aware and ready for the most cataclysmic event that will face every person on our planet, in the history of the Universe, the end of the **six thousand years of God's demonstration of His amazing LOVE for all His Creation.**

Just in my lifetime, as I have shown in Chapter 12, **"increase of knowledge and men running to and fro",** (Daniel 12:1-4), are incredible signs that Daniel was shown. These signs indicate clearly that we are at the point of **"Almost Harvest Time".** The **door of the Ark as in Noah's time**, is about to close, and the **fire that destroyed Sodom and Gomorrah** is about to happen to this sad, sinful world that we live in today. The **stone that is cut out without hands** and smashes the image of the Kingdoms of this earth, is about to happen and **God's everlasting kingdom is about to be set up, with no more kingdoms to follow,** as in Daniel's vision in chapter 2 of his book. The time of opportunity to accept **God's gift of LOVE**, the **time of probation** is about to close.

All the signs of "the end of this world", that Jesus spoke about in Matthew 24, Mark 13, and Luke 21, in answer to His disciples' questions, are very rapidly fulfilling. All the events that John speaks about in the book of Revelation, are right in front of us! The "edge of the cliff" is just ahead!

God is calling, nay, shouting to us, to **"Get ready! Get Ready! Get Ready!"**

How do we get ready? *Simply speak to God in prayer and tell Him that you love Him, and that you have <u>chosen</u> to accept His marvellous gift of salvation. Ask Him to make you clean and write your name in His Book of Life.* Like the slave at the auction market, when he realized what the buyer had done for him, paying such a high price to set him free, responded, **"Oh Master! Thank you! Thank you! Thank you! I will serve you all the days of my life!"**

In John 6:37-40 is Jesus' promise, to all who **choose** to come to Him. **"Him that cometh to Me, I will in no wise cast out."**

In Matthew 11: 28-30 Jesus says, **"Come unto Me all ye that labour and are heavy laden, and I will give you rest."**

And of course, one of the most wonderful Scriptures in God's Word, so often quoted, John 3:16,17. **"For God so loved the world that he gave His only begotten Son, that whosoever believeth in Him should not perish, but have everlasting life. For God sent not His Son into the world, to condemn the world, but that the world through Him might be saved."**

Let's continue to look at the signs He has given us of what is ahead.

The abomination of desolation, (spoken of by Daniel the Prophet, in chapter 12:11), and Jesus himself, in Matthew 24:15, **is about to be set up in Jerusalem,** *"the holy place, between the seas in the glorious holy mountain."* (Matthew 24:15, and Daniel 11:45). The Courtyard is to be taken over by the Gentiles. (World Leaders). Revelation 11:1,2.

Jesus says, "When the **abomination of desolation is** set up, **(the New World Order, man ruling the world"),** they will be in charge for **forty-two literal months**. (Revelation 11:2)

As Daniel, and Jesus Himself tell us, there will be a **"time of trouble such as never was since there was a nation."** (Daniel 12:1, and Matthew 24:21,22

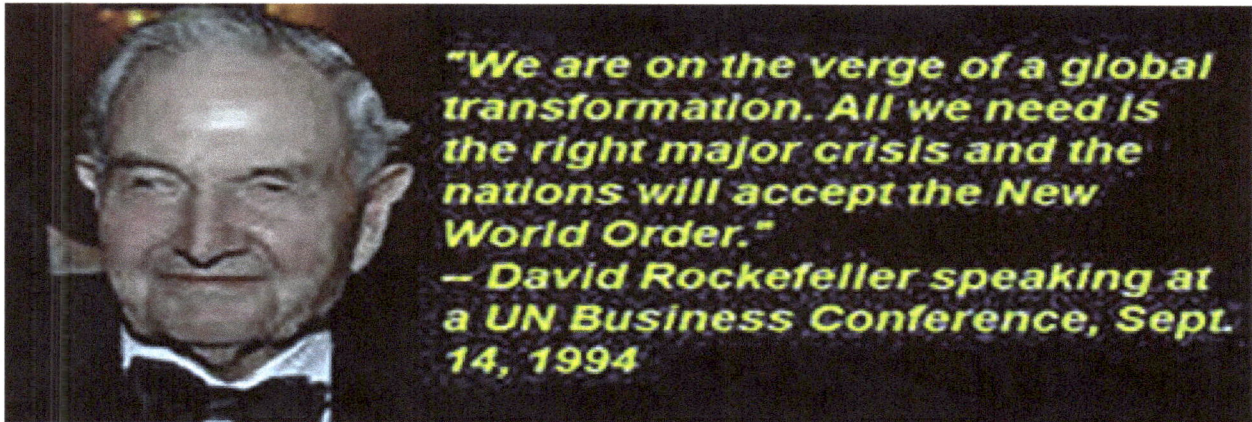

"We are on the verge of a global transformation. All we need is the right major crisis and the nations will accept the New World Order." – David Rockefeller speaking at a UN Business Conference, Sept. 14, 1994

We are seeing and hearing about this plan nearly every day on the News. As you can see from the picture, it has been planned for many years now. The picture and quote from Rockefeller is dated **1994**!

The forty-two months is exactly the same time, twelve hundred and sixty literal days, (42 X 30 =1260), **that the Two Witnesses have in Revelation 11:3,** *the very next verse!* They witness to the world at the same time the Gentiles take over the Courtyard of the Temple and rule the world setting up the **New World Order.** Perhaps this is how the **"Gospel will go to all the world….. and then the end will come!",** through these **Two Witnesses, witnessing together with God's faithful people.**

Some people are adamant that no one knows when the end will be for this world, and they quote Matthew 24:36 to support their belief. However, in the original text the word used there can mean **"makes known"**, as well as **"knows"**, which gives this text a much clearer meaning! Because Jesus is also God and One with the Father, (John 1:1, and John17:21-23), *of course* Jesus would know when the close of probation will be, *but it is the Father Who will make the announcement!*

Let me emphasize, **"No man "makes known" the day or the hour of the close of probation and Jesus' second coming, not even the angels, nor the Son, but only the Father."** Matthew 24:36. *Only the Father will "make known", (make the announcement), when His grace will end, and says, "Enough! Demonstration ended!"*

As I have pointed out in Chapter 5, what a witness it would be to the world, if the Two Tablets of the Ten Commandments, still hidden in the Ark of the Covenant in a cave under Skull Hill, would be brought forth by God Who gave them to Moses on Mt Sinai so long ago, but recently discovered by Ron Wyatt. (See Chapters 3-6).

With the two stone tablets with God's immutable Law inscribed on them by God's own fiery finger on display to the world, what a witness that would be to the Truth of God's Word, and the vital importance of the Sabbath Commandment identifying Who God is, and what day is the real seventh day of the week; the Holy Seventh-day Sabbath, that God said to **"Remember"**! What a witness it would be, with Moses holding them in his hands before the World, with every TV camera in the world focussed on them, showing them clearly, world-wide!

What a Witness that would be with Elijah shouting to the world as he did on Mount Carmel, "If Baal, (Satan), be God, then serve him, but if God be God, then serve Him." 1Kings 18:16-45.

Read how Elijah challenged the seven hundred prophets of Baal. They danced, sang, yelled out, and cut themselves, calling on Baal to burn their offerings, while Elijah mocked them; **"Call louder! Perhaps he is asleep!"** Eventually the prophets of Baal became exhausted, and **no fire had burnt their offerings!**

Then before Ahab, and all the crowd of people gathered there to witness the challenge, **Elijah prayed and asked God to burn his offering and immediately God sent fire from the heavens and consumed not only the offering, but the altar, the wood, and even the water that was brought up from the sea to fill a trench around the altar**! Read the whole exciting account of Elijah's challenge in 1 Kings 18, which is an amazing record of **Elijah's faithful Witness!** Another example of, **"the greatest want of the world! Men who will stand for the right though the heavens fall, and who are not afraid to call sin by its right name!"**

Note how these texts of Scripture in Revelation even identify who the **Two Witnesses** are! Revelation 11:3-6. One Witness can control the rain and is obviously **Elijah** who stopped the rain in the time of King Ahab, for three and a half years! I Kings 17:1. **Three and a half years is 1260 days, or forty-two months!**

Elijah telling Ahab there would be no rain, according to his word.

Elijah did not die, as we all have to die, but was taken up to heaven without dying. 2 Kings 2:11.

The other Witness, obviously **Moses**, can turn water to blood, and bring all manner of plagues upon men. Read the whole account in Exodus chapters 7-10 for the first nine plagues, and Exodus 11-13 for the tenth one. In Chapter 7: 17,18, at God's command, Moses smote the waters with his rod and the rivers were turned to blood, and nine more plagues followed, before Pharoah gave his permission for the Hebrews to leave Egypt.

the 10 Plagues

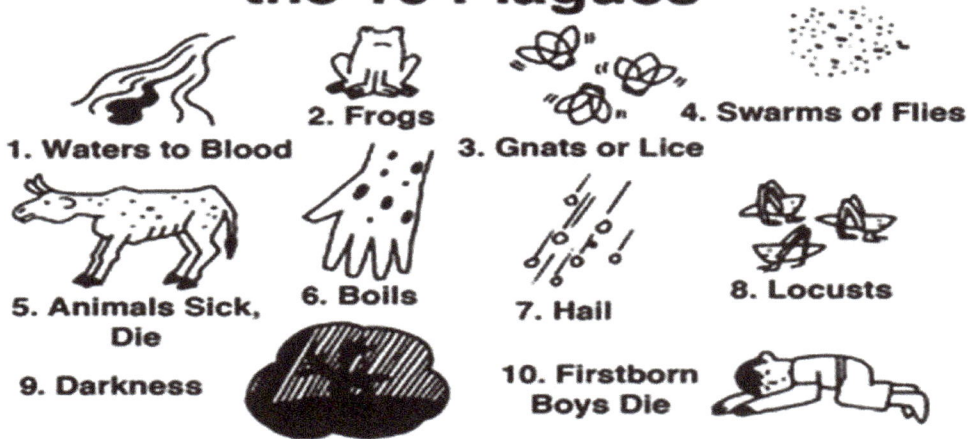

1. Waters to Blood
2. Frogs
3. Gnats or Lice
4. Swarms of Flies
5. Animals Sick, Die
6. Boils
7. Hail
8. Locusts
9. Darkness
10. Firstborn Boys Die

The Ten Plagues on Egypt.

Moses eventually died, as we all may have to do, but in Jude 1:9, Michael the Archangel raised Moses' body from the dead, and obviously took him to heaven, for we read in Matthew 17:1-6 that both Moses and Elijah stood with Jesus on the Mount of Transfiguration.

According to the Word of God, we may see **Moses and Elijah** visit our earth again, as the **Two Witnesses,** as in Revelation 11:3, for the same time period as the **Gentiles,** (the mega-rich men of this world; the rulers of the New World Order), govern the world? It's a very interesting scenario to consider, and it seems to me to be clearly what the Scriptures are telling us!

When Paul describes Jesus' second coming, in 1 Thessalonians 4:13-18, he says the dead will rise first, (represented by **Moses who <u>died</u> and was raised to life**), and then those who are alive and remain, (represented by **Elijah who was taken to Heaven <u>without dying</u>),** will be taken up to heaven, and so shall we ever be with the Lord.

Isn't our Heavenly Father amazing? We all will go **together** to meet the Lord at His Second Coming! How wonderful is our incredibly loving God Who has arranged everything well ahead to illustrate His **LOVE?** What an amazing Father to have, who leaves nothing to chance. He has a plan and knows exactly how each part of His plan is going to work out before it happens! How He can do this is beyond my simple brain to comprehend, He is the **"Eternally Existing Being"** Who **"speaks and it is done: Who commands, and it stands fast."** Psalms 33:9.

He is omnipotent, (He is all powerful!). **He is omniscient,** (He knows everything!) and **He is omnipresent,** (He is everywhere at once!) I cannot comprehend such a Being! It is far beyond my human intelligence!

Just to think of His incredible **LOVE**, and what He was willing to do, to offer salvation to all who **choose** to **"Trust and Obey"** Him, as the Hymn says, makes me very emotional and brings me to tears, every time I think about His **"Amazing Grace".** Won't you join me and accept His incredible **LOVE** for us?

There's no handle on the outside of this door!

When Jesus knocks, *you have to choose*

to open the door and invite Jesus to come in!

Yes, it is truly all about LOVE!

CHAPTER 37

PREPARATION FOR THE FINAL CRISIS

As I write this it is toward the end of 2024 AD, and the signs Daniel and Jesus spoke about regarding the "time of the end", "the end of the world", as outlined in chapter 12 of this book, are happening in rapid succession. We, in Australia and New Zealand, are living in comparative luxury when we see what is happening in so many other parts of our world such as has been going on now for years in Russia and Ukraine. The terrible atrocities happening in the Middle East could well escalate into World War 3. All countries of the world are becoming involved. This could well be the beginning of the **"time of trouble such as never was since there was a nation".** Daniel 12 and Matthew 24.

Could this be the beginning of **"the right major crisis that will prompt the nations of the world to accept the New World Order,** as in the quote from David Rockefeller that I have already shown in Chapter 34?

If the mega-rich World Leaders, decide to set up a New World Government, to fix all the problems of the world, as United Nations leaders have been planning for some years, could this be the fulfilment of the Word of the prophet John in Revelation chapter 11:1 and 2, where the **Gentile nations take over the "courtyard" of the Holy City and tread it down underfoot for 42 months? (1260 days, a literal three and a half years)?**

So, what is **God's Holy City**, which is located **"Between the seas"**, (the Mediterranean and the Dead Sea,) **"in the glorious Holy Mountain"**, (Mount Moriah, the Temple Mount, physically purchased by Abraham, from Ephron for 400 shekels of silver? (See Genesis 23, for this Real Estate deal.)

The only city I know of that fits this description is **JERUSALEM.**

Are the New World Order leaders of the United Nations, planning their headquarters to be set up in Jerusalem? Who is the most popular man on earth who could lead such a worldwide government? We are told that only those who have the Mark of this beast power, will be able to buy or sell. Hmmm!

Could the Mark or seal of this power be Sunday worship? Could it be that this great world power will require everyone on earth to receive its **Mark**, or be exterminated? Wouldn't it be another example of **Force** rather than **Love**?

Are you and I ready as much as we can be, and willing, like the three Hebrew boys, who told Nebuchadnezzar that they would not bow down to any other god or image, other than the God of Heaven, no matter what maybe the consequences? We are seeing already, so many of our Heavenly Father's faithful people, suffering horrible persecution in many parts of our world.

"The greatest want of the world is men and women who are so close to God that they will stand for the right though the heavens fall"! *Do you and I love our Heavenly Father enough to worship and obey Him, no matter what the consequences may be, even unto death?*

Why has God told us about all this before it happens? Could it be that He wants His people to be prepared as much as possible for this "time of trouble"? That's what any loving parent would do, isn't it? Just another example of His Infinite Love!

Most of all we must make sure our **"noses are off the ground, and not like the hounds chasing the Tasmanian Wolf"**, as in the Chapter 10 **"True Australian Story"**, "unaware that the cliff face was not very far ahead."

Let's not be like the people in Noah's day who **"were eating and drinking, marrying and giving in marriage, chasing money, houses and lands and the pleasures of this life, until the flood came and took them all away."** See Matthew 24:36-39

The opportunity to avoid eternal death is still available! The offer of eternal life with God in an earth made new is still available. This wonderful gift from our God, Who is LOVE, is *fully paid for* and available to all who will <u>choose</u> to accept His LOVE!

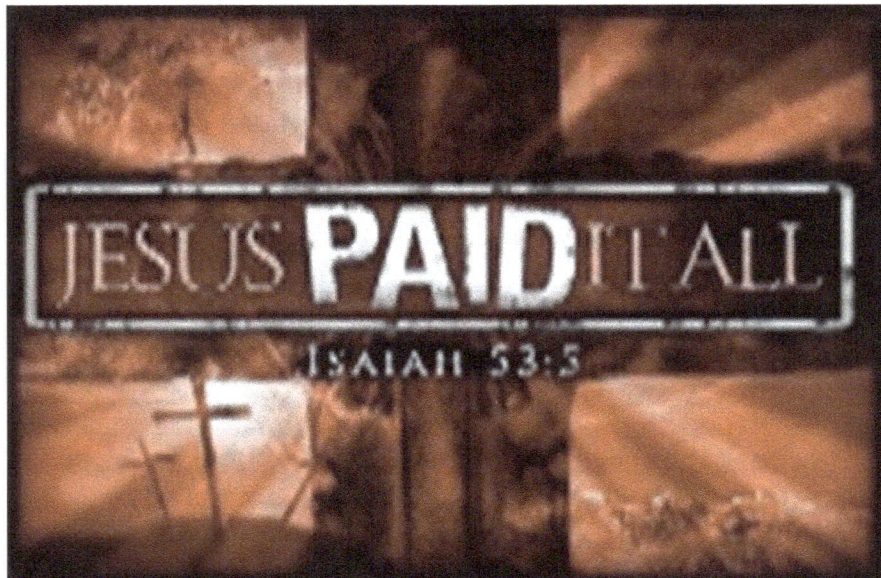

No mortgage! Nothing owing! Just a free gift of LOVE

CHAPTER 38

PREPARE FOR WHAT IS SURELY COMING

In this chapter are some worthwhile suggestions to think about, which could help us to cope with this "time of trouble", as much as possible, till we have to depend totally on God "for manna to eat and water from a rock to drink." Please feel free to share these ideas with your family and friends and whoever will listen.

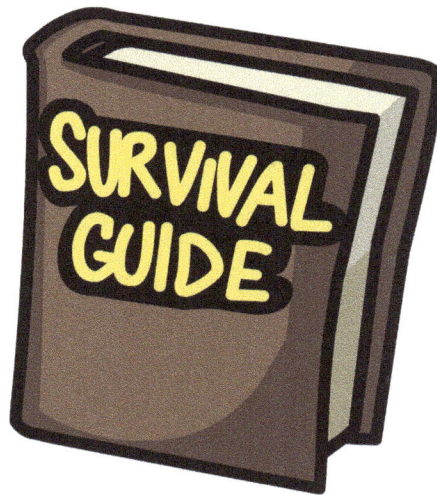

With what we see happening in our world today, many people realize that we are on the verge of a major Economic Collapse and will soon be entering another Great Depression, and "a Time of Trouble such as never was since the world began." But only a small percentage of those same people are prepared for that to happen. The sad truth is that the vast majority of people would last little more than a month on what they have stored up in their homes. Most of us are so used to running out to the Supermarket or to many other stores for whatever we need, that we never even stop to consider what would happen if suddenly we were not able to do that.

Already the economy is beginning to stumble about like a drunken fat boy. Major wars are happening right now, in a number of regions such as in Ukraine and Russia, and the Middle East, which could quickly escalate into World War Three. Thousands of innocent people, even women, children and the elderly are being massacred. China is flexing its muscles to take Taiwan. There is serious unrest in so many other parts of our world.

"Natural" disasters such as earthquakes, famines, droughts, fires, hurricanes, tornadoes, floods, and horrible crimes are happening more and more, with millions of people without the necessities of life. We are seeing it happening right here in Australia, right now as I write this very timely message and warning to all who have ears to listen.

So just how would you survive if you suddenly could not rely on the huge international corporate giants to feed, clothe and supply you and your family with your daily needs? Do you have a plan?

Unless you already live in a cave or you are a complete and total mindless follower of the establishment media, you should be able to see very clearly that our society is more vulnerable now than it ever has been. Unprecedented numbers of large earthquakes around the world and volcanoes are erupting all over the globe. Just take a look at what has happened in Turkey, in Morocco, in Afghanistan to see how devastating these natural disasters can be. Not only that, but we have a world that is full of lunatics in positions of power, and if one of them decides to set off a nuclear, chemical or biological weapon in a major city it could paralyse an entire region.

The War in the Middle East right now will make the price of Oil double or triple (at least), with the likelihood of no fuel supplies at all being available. We depend so much on the Middle East for Oil supplies!

There is the possibility that much of the entire world could be drawn into the conflict. Scientists tell us that a massive high-altitude EMP blast, (Electro Magnetic Pulse), could send large portions of the world back to the stone age in an instant. In addition, there is the constant threat that another outbreak of a major viral pandemic, (such as what happened with the world-wide COVID pandemic), which could kill tens of millions of people around the globe and paralyse the economies of the world. But even without all of that, the truth is that the economy of most countries is going to collapse. So just think of what will happen if one (or more) of these things mentioned above, does happen on top of all the economic problems that we are having.

Are you and I as ready as possible for this coming crisis? Here are some very interesting and helpful suggestions from a book I read recently:

20 things you and your family will need, to survive:

1. Storable Food

Food is going to instantly become one of the most valuable commodities in existence in the event of an economic collapse, and major crisis. If you do not have food, you are not going to survive. Most present-day families could not last much longer than a month on what they have in their homes right now. So, what about you? If disaster struck right now, how long could you survive on what you have?

The truth is that we all need to start storing up food, dried, in cans or bottled. If you and your family run out of food, you will suddenly find yourselves competing with the hordes of hungry people who are looting the stores and roaming the streets looking for something to eat. Of course, you can grow your own food, but that is going to take time. So, you need to have enough food stored up until the food that you plant has time to grow. But if you have not stored up any seeds you might as well forget it. When the economy totally collapses, the remaining seeds will disappear very quickly. So, if you think that you are going to need seeds, now is the time to get them.

2. Clean Water

Most people can survive for a number of weeks without food, but without water you will die in just a few days. So where would you get water if the water suddenly stopped flowing out of your taps? Do you have a plan? Is there an abundant supply of clean water near your home? Would you be able to boil water if you need to?

Besides storing water and figuring out how you are going to gather water if society breaks down, another thing to consider is water purification tablets. The water you are able to gather during a time of crisis may not be suitable for drinking. So you may find that water purification tablets come in very, very handy.

3. Shelter

You can't sleep on the streets, can you? Well, some people will be able to get by living on the streets, as some are doing already, right here in Australia, because they can't afford to continue paying mortgage or rent, but the vast majority of us will need some form of shelter to survive for long. So, what would you do if you and your family lost your home or suddenly were forced from your home?

Where would you go? The best thing to do is to come up with several plans. Do you have relatives that you can bunk with in case of emergency? Do you own a tent and sleeping bags if you had to rough it? If one day everything hits the fan and you and your family have to "bug out" somewhere, where would that be? You need to have a plan.

4. Warm Clothing

If you plan to survive for long in a nightmare situation, you are probably going to need some warm, functional clothing. If you live in a cold climate, this is going to mean storing up plenty of blankets and cold weather clothes. If you live in an area where-it rains a lot, you will need to be sure to store up some rain gear. If you think you may have to survive outdoors in an emergency situation, make sure that you and your family have something warm to wear.

Someday after the initial troubles have started and people are scrambling to survive, a lot of folks are going to end up freezing to death. In fact, in the coldest areas it is actually possible to freeze to death in your own home. Don't let that happen to you.

5. An Axe or Tomahawk and Bush Knife

Staying along the theme of staying warm, you may want to consider investing in a good axe or at least a Tomahawk or Bush Knife. In the event of a major emergency, gathering firewood will be a priority. Without a good tool to cut the wood, it would be much more difficult.

6. Lighters or Matches

You will also want something to start a fire with. If you can start a fire, you can cook food, you can boil water and you can stay warm. So, in a true emergency situation, how do you plan to start a fire? By rubbing sticks together? Now is the time to put away a supply of lighters or matches so that you will be prepared when you really need them.

In addition, you may want to consider storing up a good supply of candles. Candles come in quite handy whenever the electricity goes out. In the event of a longer nightmare, we will all see why our forefathers relied on candles so much.

7. Hiking Boots or Comfortable Shoes

When you ask most people to list things necessary for survival, this is not the first or the second thing that comes to mind. But having hiking boots or very comfortable and functional shoes will be absolutely critical. You may very well find yourself in a situation where you and your family must walk everywhere you want to go. So how far do you think you will get in high heels? You will want footwear that you would feel comfortable walking in for hours if necessary. You will also want footwear that will last a long time, because when the economy truly collapses you may not be able to run out to the shoe store and get what you need at that point.

8. A Flashlight and or Lantern

When the power goes off in your home, what is the first thing that you grab? Just think about it. A flashlight or a lantern of course. In a major emergency a Flashlight or a Lantern will be a necessity - especially if you need to go anywhere at night.

Solar powered or "crank style" flashlights or lanterns will probably be best during a long-term emergency. If you have battery-powered units you will want to begin storing lots of batteries.

9. A Radio

If a major crisis does happen, what will you and your family want? Among other things, you will all want to know what in the world is going on. A Radio can be an invaluable tool for keeping up with the news. Once again, solar powered or "crank style" radios will probably work best for the long term. A battery-powered unit would work as well - but only for as long as your batteries are able to last.

10. Communication Equipment

When things really hit the fan, you are going to want to communicate with your family and friends. You will also want to be able to contact an ambulance or law enforcement if necessary.

Having an emergency cell phone is great, but it may or may not work during a time of crisis. The Internet also may or may not be available. Be sure to have a plan (whether it be high-tech or low-tech), for staying in communication with others during a major emergency.

11. A Swiss Army Knife

If you have ever owned a Swiss Army knife, you probably already know how incredibly handy they can be. It can be a very valuable and versatile tool. In a true survival situation, a Swiss Army knife can literally do dozens of different things for you. Make sure that you have at least one stored up for emergencies.

12. Personal Hygiene Items

While these may not be absolute "essentials", the truth is that life will get very unpleasant very quickly without them. For example, what would you do without toilet paper? Just think about it. Imagine that you just finished your last roll of toilet paper and now you can't get any more. What would you do?

The truth is that soap, toothbrushes, toothpaste, shampoo, toilet paper and other hygiene products are things that we completely take for granted in society today. So, what would happen if we could not go out and buy them any longer?

13. A First Aid Kit and Other Medical Supplies

On a more serious note, you may not be able to access a hospital or a doctor during a major crisis. In your survival supplies, be absolutely certain that you have a good first aid kit and any other medical supplies that you think you may need.

14. Extra Gasoline

There may come a day when gasoline is rationed or is simply not available at all. If that happens, how will you get around? Be certain to have some extra gasoline stored away just in case you find yourself really needing to get somewhere someday, and you can't just fill-up at the bowser!

15. A Sewing Kit

If you were not able to run out and buy new clothes for you and your family, what would you do? Well, you would want to repair the clothes that you have and make them last as long as possible. Without a good sewing kit that will be very difficult to do.

16. Self-Defence Equipment

Whether it is pepper spray to fend off wild animals or something more "robust" to fend off wild humans, millions of Australians, and other people, will one day be thankful that they have something to defend themselves with.

17. A Compass

In the event of a major emergency, you and your family may find yourselves having to be on the move. If you are in a wilderness area, it will be very hard to tell what direction you are heading without a compass. It is always a good idea to have at least one compass stored up.

18. A Hiking Backpack

If you and your family suddenly must "bug out", what will you carry all of your survival supplies in? Having a good hiking backpack or "survival bag" for everyone in your family is extremely important. If something happened in the city where you live and you suddenly had to "go", what would you put your most important stuff in? How would you carry it all if you had to travel by foot? These are very important things to think about.

19. A Community

During a long-term crisis, it is those who are willing to work together that will have the best chance of making it. Whether it is your family, your friends, a church, or a local group of people that you know, make sure that you have some people that you can rely on and work together with in the event that everything "hits the fan". Loners are going to have a really hard time of surviving for long.

20. A Backup Plan

Lastly, it is always, always, always important to have a backup plan for everything. If someone comes in and steals all the food that you have stored up, what are you going to do?

If travel is restricted and you can't get to your "bug out" location immediately, do you have a Plan B?

If you have built your house into an impregnable survival fortress but circumstances force you to leave do you have an alternate plan?

The truth is that crisis situations rarely unfold just as we envision. It is important to be flexible and to be ready with backup plans when disaster strikes.

You don't want to end up like the folks in Darwin after Cyclone Tracy, in 1974, with 60% of Darwin's houses destroyed, and only 6% left still habitable. You don't want to have to rely on the government to take care of you if something really bad happens. We've had severe bushfires on the tablelands near Toowoomba, severe flooding in Tasmania, Victoria, and New South Wales, and in the Lockyer Valley in Queensland.

Right now, the strategic grain reserves are not sufficient to feed approximately 27 million people in Australia for very long. How long do you think that is going to last?

Incredibly hard times are imminent! Would you be able to survive when it happens? For most people it will be an overwhelming surprise!

Now is the time to be prepared and make the Lord our safe haven. Are you ready for a "time of trouble such as never was since there was a nation", as the prophet Daniel says is coming in Daniel 12, and Jesus Himself says in Matthew 24?

Now is the time to GET READY! GET READY! GET READY! Now is the time to PREPARE! Now is the time to be right with God, and stand true to Him, no matter what the cost!

He is an incredible Being with such love that is too far beyond me to understand. Won't you join me in loving and serving Him?

Psalm 91 shows God's LOVE for His people in times of crisis.

CHAPTER 39

HEALTH OF BODY, MIND AND SPIRIT

"Without Health the richest man is poor!"

So many people are ignorant of how to care for their bodies for optimum physical health, mental health and spiritual health. I'd like now to share some important truths regarding these important areas of our lives.

Our hearts are seriously heavy when we see the suffering and disease so prevalent in society today. We have experienced suffering and illness ourselves but have found sound basic principles that have helped us greatly in our search for optimum health.

Sometimes, just a simple change in diet and/or habits can have a profound benefit. For example, as a young man, I suffered terribly for many years with severe Asthma. Simply giving up dairy products, which, by the way, I loved to consume, caused the Asthma to disappear permanently almost overnight! All the medications and puffers I was using eased the symptoms but did nothing to eradicate what was causing the problem.

I grew up like most Aussies following the Standard Australian Diet–the SAD plan. At fifteen years old, I suffered a serious attack of Appendicitis, but thanks to a wise old doctor, I still have my appendix today over 70 years later. Doc ordered **"NIL BY MOUTH–WATER ONLY"** and in three days the pain was gone, and he sent me home with strict instructions—- "Make it a habit", he said, "to empty the rubbish every morning!" I took his advice and have never had another attack!

These early experiences inspired me to do serious research into the principles our wonderful Creator put into place to keep our bodies operating at optimum efficiency.

We believe there is definitely a place for skilled medical people in cases of accident and trauma. I, for one, would not be here today without the help of skilled surgeons who put me together again after a highly revving chainsaw ripped through my right chest. However, the use of drugs to treat lifestyle diseases can exacerbate the problems, causing untold suffering and death in many, many instances. In the USA alone, every year, over a quarter of a million people die from doctor-prescribed medications.

When doctors graduated, they used to pledge the Hippocratic Oath–**FIRST DO NO HARM!** Hippocrates, hailed as the Father of Medicine also says: **"Let food be your medicine, and medicine be your food!"**

Let's consider these basic Eight Laws of Health.

"N E W S T A R T" is a pneumonic that helps us remember them:

Nutrition, **E**xercise, **W**ater, **S**unshine, **T**emperance, **A**ir, **R**est, **T**rust in Divine Power.

NUTRITION

Fruits, nuts, grains and vegetables, prepared in as simple a manner as possible, free from grease! This is the simple basic recipe.

One only has to observe the shopping carts in supermarkets to see how people are eating large quantities of processed, refined, packaged foods and drinks. These have high amounts of sugar, flavourings and chemicals are used to preserve what would otherwise spoil quickly. More and more people today are overweight, and suffering all sorts of nasty diseases as the body tries to eliminate toxic substances in our food, water and air.

Even fresh fruits and vegetables grown commercially are sprayed with insecticides, fungicides, pesticides, hormones, and preservative compounds before they reach consumers. Many of our foods are genetically modified with potential serious effects for consumers. We feel it is a good practice to learn how to read the labels on foods and find out what the sections and contents mean. Learning to leave a product on the shelf takes practice at first.

There is a very handy pocket-sized booklet which we have found very helpful and very easy to use, to note what is in different products, and to check what all those numbers in the ingredients mean and their side effects. It is called, **"The Chemical Maze"** by Bill Statham. **"Your guide to FOOD ADDITIVES and COSMETIC INGREDIENTS."**

In developed countries, **Flesh Foods** have often become the norm. It is fair to say that since the arrival of fast-food chains, TV dinners and the like, people have become unhealthier over time. Disease, obesity and ill-health is increasing at an alarming rate today! Obesity rates are a leading problem even with our children. Medical practitioners may offer good advice; however, the remedy is often very simple.

Put the right fuel into your "body machine". We are what we eat!

I have personally tried to care for my body, by using only **Plant-based foods** for nearly seventy years, since my early twenties, and still enjoy relatively good health.

Let's think about how we may stop flooding our system with toxic chemicals or harming our bodies with other habits, including "social drugs", that actually destroy the body you were given, with disease and ultimately death. Medical drugs, used so often today to treat lifestyle diseases, just cover symptoms instead of dealing with the cause of the problems. **"LET FOOD BE YOUR MEDICINE, AND MEDICINE BE YOUR FOOD!"** is the advice of Hippocrates, the "father of medicine."

We realise organic products costs more, but there may be choices we can make on the shopping list – such as organic milk rather than regular milk or replacing dairy with almond or other non-dairy milks on breakfast cereals. These are small but decisive steps in contrast to no steps at all. They add up over time. **What price do we put on good health?**

Another conscious choice we can make is to use pure Australian Olive Oil and particularly Coconut Oil, rather than other vegetable oils or animal fats. We can stay away from all deep-fried foods and try to include "greens" with our meals. This is not to say we can be perfect or adjust to all things at once, but it is a worthwhile change to our pattern of behaviour, which will benefit our overall health.

Then of course, is the topic of how we prepare and eat our foods. If we are tuned into change, we will come across simple food preparation methods one by one. For example, instead of boiling our greens we can lightly pan fry with some garlic or real ginger and Coconut Oil. We can make great salads with more finely chopped raw ingredients and spread some avocado on rice biscuits.

What this implies is some understanding of how we use our time. The time it takes to drive for a take-away could be used to prepare foods on the chopping board. Instead of working on the computer till six at night, we can stop at five, relax a little, and prepare a rewarding meal. A good place to begin is by purchasing delicious **organic fruits and vegetables, or if possible**, grow your own for our required vitamins and minerals.

Nuts of many kinds provide wonderful unprocessed oils and nutrients for the whole body. As an example, when we first changed from salted nuts and sweets to plant- based foods and raw nuts, it didn't take too long for our sense of taste to adjust.

When we return to old habits such as soft drink, or use the same amount of refined salt, we may not want it anymore as it is too strong.

It is quite easy to try out raw foods such as chopping mushrooms into a salad. Next time you buy a stick of corn, try slicing off the corn into the salad bowl. Explore the taste of raw foods. Chomp into a crisp green bean. It takes a little while to adjust but is very rewarding health-wise.

EXERCISE

Daily exercise is essential to energise and invigorate body and mind. We are made to move. Healthy people have various routines that work for them. One way is to start on some walks or use the local gym without over-extending yourself or doing moves that are not natural to the body. A good trainer can give lots of invaluable insight for mixing your workouts with body movements and machines if you like that approach.

Exercise involves blood and oxygen circulation – aerobics. There are recommended practices for breathing and heart rate. Regular exercise stimulates the body's systems to work at more optimum levels. It is wonderful if you are near a beach and can connect with the earth's magnetic fields, by walking barefoot on the sand, and enjoying the ocean water, swimming or surfing.

There are many options for us to have physical exercise – even a Skipping Rope. riding a bicycle, hiking, playing sports, using a Trampoline, attending a Gym, general daily work, gardening. These are some activities to help the mind and body to be healthy and can be fun too.

WATER

Our bodies are 45% to 65% water. Body fat contains approximately 10 percent water, while muscle is approximately 75 percent water. We need to re-hydrate regularly during the day. Sometimes people think they are hydrated, but are not – for example, change in voice tone, heat stroke and so on. Drinks that dehydrate contain caffeine, such as that "cuppa" (Coffee or Tea), we as Aussies love. It is helpful to drink good quality water throughout the day. Perhaps add a touch of lemon or lime. Good water is "smooth" and pleasant to the taste.

It varies how much people are willing to drink. For example, one can make a habit of a glass or two of water before breakfast and during the day. Some people drink bottles of water during the day, as they move about in their work jobs. For ourselves, we try to drink six to eight glasses of water every day, especially if we are unable to get raw foods on a particular day. When we use uncooked raw foods, we obtain much higher water-content in the food. Aim for a high percentage of raw foods. For example, 70-80%, for optimum vitality.

Cooking removes much of the goodness in foods, especially the live enzymes. Live food is essential for maximising vitality. Life and vitality come from living food. We can't get abundant life force from food that is dead! Try cooking seeds before you plant your garden, and what will happen? The life force is gone, and there's no response or growth! **The life force is gone**!

Lots of clean pure water is essential to good health. Review your local water supplies and the chemicals added, especially sodium fluoride and chlorine. Pets and plants need clean, pure water too. Town or city water can be put through good quality filters to remove bacteria, but it is very difficult to remove the chemicals used in most town waters today. Rainwater tanks can provide chemical-free water especially out in country areas, but there still may be many chemicals in the air which can fall down with the rain.

SUNSHINE

Daily exposure of the skin to sunshine promotes health. Sunshine really boosts the immune system. Vitamin D is produced by the action of sunlight on the skin. Work out which are the best times in your region for morning and afternoon sun exposure.

Too much sun causes burns and severe discomfort. You may protect your skin with long sleeves, trousers and a hat. In high-sunshine areas it is really necessary to wear a hat outdoors. Review the sunscreens on the market for longer term use. We once saw this label – **"Prolonged use may cause cancer."** Use sunscreens that are made from natural ingredients.

Energy from the sun every day, promotes life and health in all living things whether in the ocean, the air or on land.

TEMPERANCE

Leaving all things harmful and using even good things in moderation! This is a great practice to follow to prevent long-term damage to the body and its cells.

Avoid completely, alcohol, tea and coffee. Refined sugar, most processed and refined foods are quite harmful to the body; care in avoiding saturated fats, cola drinks and other soft drinks; follow strategies to remove addictions and life-style dependencies on these foods, and particularly for alcohol, tea, coffee, tobacco, and drugs.

In our home we use many lovely herbal teas. We especially like dandelion, liquorice and peppermint. We use raw honey or maple syrup for a sweetener. Be careful not to overwork. Take time to rest and enjoy your family, friends and the beautiful things of nature, which can still be found and enjoyed in our world. For those of us who consider God as our Maker, we take rest on the seventh-day Sabbath, and take time out to commune and pray in a special way with our Maker on His special day as in Genesis 1 and 2 of the Scriptures. Try a diary and change any harmful habits.

AIR

Pure air is essential for good health. Breathing deeply every day will flood the cells with fresh life-giving oxygen. Try some deep breathing while exercising different muscle groups of the body. The brain needs oxygenated blood to enable clear thinking and a happy attitude. Even in winter it is good to have some fresh air flowing through one's sleeping area.

Of course, country air, where there are lots of trees, has much better oxygen content than air in towns and cities. Enjoy the fresh air outdoors and the beauty of natural surroundings to lift your spirit and oxygenate your cells. Walks at the beach or through a forest are very helpful.

A simple exercise to boost Oxygen intake, is to do the **"777"** breathing plan often during the day or night.

Breathe in slowly for seven seconds to fill the lungs; hold for seven seconds, and then slowly breathe out for seven seconds.

Repeat the exercise as often as comfortable.

REST

During sound sleep the cells of the body are repaired, re-energised, and wastes removed. Normally we need six to eight hours of sound sleep each night. If you suffer from disturbed sleep, check your habits, and make any necessary changes.

Some old but good sayings to remember are, **"An hour's sleep before midnight is worth two hours after"**, or **"Early to bed and early to rise, makes a man happy, healthy and wise."**

Our bodies operate in what scientists call **Circadian Rhythms**.

From about noon to 8pm in the evening each day, are the eight hours of **"INTAKE"** cycle.

From 8 pm to 4 am is the "REPAIR" cycle – no snacks at this time! The hormone melatonin is produced during this time of night. It helps promote sound sleep.

From 4 am to noon is the "WASTE" cycle.

These are only approximate times. They can vary and be changed by our patterns or habits. Sleep recharges our batteries, to be ready for the next day. We need rest, recreation, holidays, and can usually tell when we need these times. We notice the effect of being weary and the need for times of rest, just as in our Christian teaching. Jesus Christ gave times of rest to the disciples – **"times to come apart from the crowds and rest a while"**. Mark 6:30-31.

We believe in a loving Creator who has designed time for us to rest and to be with Him and honour Him, especially on His seventh-day Sabbath. Many practitioners of health, artists, and people from all walks of life know of benefit from time with God.

TRUST IN OUR CREATOR

I am fearfully and wonderfully made! The human body has in-built abilities to heal itself! Really, they are outstanding!

Be sure to read my amazing story, **"TRUST AND OBEY AND LIVE"** in an earlier chapter.

The "body machine" is indeed very remarkable in God's creation. The more I study how it works, the more I exclaim with King David, **"I am fearfully and wonderfully made!"** Psalm 139:14 – All praise to our omniscient Creator! Our God is everywhere. His ear is not so heavy that He cannot hear whenever we need Him. He **"never slumbers nor sleeps."** Psalm 121:4

Sometimes He says, **"Wait a while"** – we just have to trust Him because, **"Above the distractions of earth He sits enthroned. All things are open to His divine survey, and from His great and calm eternity, He orders that which His providence sees best."** Ministry of Healing page 239.

"Prayer is the opening of the heart to God as to a Friend". "Why should the sons and daughters of God be reluctant to pray, when prayer is the key in the Hand of Faith, to unlock Heaven's Storehouse where are treasured the boundless resources of Omnipotence." Steps to Christ page 94.

How important is our health to you and to me? It is incredibly important because **"Without health, the richest man is poor!"**

Some references to health from the Scriptures are:

"What? Know ye not that your body is the temple of the Holy Ghost which is in you, which ye have of God, and ye are not your own? 1 Corinthians 6:19

"For ye are bought with a price: therefore, glorify God in your body, and in your spirit, which are God's." 1 Corinthians 6:20

"Whether therefore ye eat, or drink, or whatsoever ye do, do all to the glory of God." 1 Corinthians 10:31

Our bodies are much more than a "machine". We have a mind, intelligence, and spirit, all designed and made for communicating with each other, and most importantly with God.

As we attend to and practice these important principles, we show a responsibility that further helps our wholeness and ability to be well with ourselves, with our Maker and with others.

When we TRUST God, worship Him, and follow His instructions as our Creator and Redeemer, we can have peace of mind, health of body, and strength of spirit.

What an amazing, loving Heavenly Father, Who we can Trust as our foundation of Truth! He has provided all our needs to get well and stay well!

Check out the many wonderful Testimonies of people who have followed God's Eight Laws of Health, at my website: www.getwellnstaywell.com

Again, it is all about our God of LOVE!

CHAPTER 40

MORE SUBTLE DECEPTIONS OF THE ENEMY

CHRISTMAS (XMAS)

Just recently, I came across some startling facts regarding Xmas, which really shocked me. I feel compelled to share what I found with you all, but what you do with these facts is entirely up to you.

Before I share anything further with you, please take your Bible and read why the enemy of God, Lucifer, is trying to imitate our true God.

Go to:

Isaiah 14:12-14. "How art thou fallen from heaven, O Lucifer, son of the morning! How art thou cut down to the ground, which did weaken the nations!

For thou hast said in thine heart, I will ascend into heaven, I will exalt my throne above the stars of God: I will sit also upon the mount of the congregation, in the sides of the north: I will ascend above the heights of the clouds: I will be like the Most High."

Lucifer, Satan, has achieved his plan so well that most of the world and many professing Christians have been deceived, and are ignorantly worshipping the enemy of our God.

Do you know that the 25th of December, is the birthday of many heathen gods?

Apollo -a Greco Roman deity! **Mithra**-a Hindu god! Horus-the Egyptian god! **Helio**-the Greek god! **Baal** and the re-incarnated **Nimrod Tammuz**! All had their birthdays at the winter solstice in the northern hemisphere---**25thDecember**. Check what God says about worshipping other gods, **Exodus 20: 3-6**. The first four of the Ten Commandments tell clearly of our relationship to our Creator. The first one simply says: **"Thou shalt have no other gods before Me."**

Do you know that Jesus could not have been born at that time of year which is the middle of winter in the Northern Hemisphere?

The shepherds were out caring for their sheep, so it could NOT have been later than about the end of October!

The **25th December** has nothing to do with Jesus' birth! It has to do with the birthdays of many pagan gods, as I've shown above, and was celebrated long before Jesus appeared, as **Saturnalia**, the re-birth of the Sun and its upward journey to the summer solstice. **It was the Roman emperor**

Constantine who brought in Xmas in 325AD. It was also called **Yule Day.** Check it out in the history books in your local library or ask Mr Google.

Do you know why people have Xmas trees in their homes?

This too stems from an ancient Luciferian custom. Egyptians worshipped the **Palm tree**, (Jeremiah 10:5), but Rome chose the **Fir tree**, which is what we see everywhere today in every mall and many front yards and insides of homes at Xmas time. Check out what God says about it in **Jeremiah 10:2-4.** He even describes how the heathen deck their trees with gold and silver ornaments!

"Thus saith the Lord. Learn not the way of the heathen and be not dismayed at the signs of heaven; for the heathen are dismayed ("terrified" NLT), at them.

For the customs of the people are vain: for one cutteth a tree out of the forest, the work of the hands of the workman, with an axe.

They deck it with silver and gold; they fasten it with nails and with hammers that it move not."

Amazing! I had never before noticed this in the Scriptures.

Do you know why Santa always has a red suit?

This really shocked me! Again, Satan has done his deceit so well.

See **Revelation 19:13.** Speaking of Jesus' return.... **"He was clothed in a vesture dipped in blood."** What colour is blood?

Do you know why his hair is white like wool?

Again, more deceit from the father of lies. John, the apostle, describing his vision of Jesus returning... **Revelation 1:14 "His head and hairs were white like wool, as white as snow.."**

Do you know why he supposedly lives at, and comes from the North Pole?

Where was the Most Holy Place in the Sanctuary? In the North side. See **Exodus 26:35 and Psalm 48:2. "Beautiful for situation, the joy of the whole earth, is mount Zion, on the sides of the North, the city of the great King."**

Do you know why he comes only once a year?

How often was the Day of Atonement? Once a year! See **Leviticus 23:28. "Also on the tenth day of the seventh month, there shall be a day of atonement..."**

Do you know how he claims to be in every home and place worldwide at the same time?

Here again, Satan is supposedly **omnipresent like God, and we never bother to see it for what it really is...total deception!** Only God has this unique attribute by His Spirit, to be everywhere present at the same time! See **Psalm 139:7-10.**

"Whither shall I go from thy spirit? Or whither shall I flee from thy presence?

If I ascend up to heaven, thou art there: if I make my bed in hell, behold thou art there.

If I take the wings of the morning, and dwell in the uttermost parts of the sea; even there shall thy hand lead me, and thy right hand shall uphold me."

Do you know why he comes saying, "Ho! Ho! Ho!"

This really shocked me too! Go to **Zechariah 2:6 "Ho! Ho! Come forth and flee from the land of the North saith the Lord…"**

Satan even copies what our returning Lord says! I had never noticed that in the Scriptures before either! How deceitful and subtle is the enemy of our God!

Do you know why he calls the little children to him?

What was Jesus' attitude toward the little children? **Luke 18:16 "Suffer the little children to come unto me and forbid them not: for of such is the kingdom of heaven."**

Do you know why he keeps coming year after year?

He claims to be eternal, having immortality like God. Only God has immortality!   **1 Timothy 1:15-17 "Now unto the King eternal, immortal, invisible, the <u>only wise God,</u> be honour and glory for ever and ever. Amen"**

Do you know why it's "Merry Christmas" and "Christmas Carols"?

Psalms 95:1 and 2. **"O come, let us sing unto the Lord: Let us make a <u>joyful noise</u> to the rock of our salvation.**

Let us come before Him with thanksgiving; Let us make a <u>joyful noise</u> unto Him with <u>psalms</u>."

How cleverly, cunningly, the great deceiver, **the father of lies** has disguised his identity and has deceived the whole world, including so many professing Christians. **Isaiah14:12-14.**

Even the name **Santa** is a clever disguise of who Lucifer really is. Just put the letter "t" in the middle and the letter "n" at the end, and you have his true identity.... **Satan.**

The above questions are just a few of thirty ways Santa counterfeits our Saviour and Lord. I have to thank **John Osborne** for opening my eyes and showing myself and Naomi, <u>**thirty ways**</u> the enemy of God tries to imitate Jesus. John had a presentation on You Tube, from which I found this information. It was:

https://www.youtube.com/watch?v=lZ9sfzcKUBk

When I tried to open it again now, I see this message:

"This video is no longer available because the YouTube account associated with this video has been terminated."

Hmmm! I wonder why??

So, when we know the Truth about Xmas, let's ask the simple question:

"O Come Let Us Worship <u>Whom</u>?"

EASTER

Easter actually began also as a pagan festival to celebrate spring in the Northern Hemisphere, long before Jesus arrived as a baby in Bethlehem.

Professor Carole Cusack of Sydney University has researched this and says that people have celebrated the equinoxes and the solstices as sacred times from ages past. Most people have no idea where these strange practices originated.

As a boy I remember Grandma Menkens hiding coloured, decorated **Easter Eggs** in and around the gardens every Easter time for us children to search and find. In pagan folklore, the eggs were supposed to remind everyone that winter was past and new life would spring into action.

This was brought into Christianity, as **"Good Friday"**, and **"Easter Sunday"**, as symbols of Jesus' death as our Saviour, and when we can have a new life, as in His resurrection, by accepting Him as our Saviour and Lord. This sounds like a valid reason for us to follow this pagan custom, but it really is just another way Satan deceives people into following his dastardly schemes and adopting pagan customs. Eastern European countries still follow this very popular custom of pagan origins, and it is happening right across the world now including here in Australia as well.

Then there are the **"Easter Rabbits and Hares",** which were associated with the goddess of fertility Eostre. These animals proliferate very quickly, with new babies happening. This pagan custom is supposed to remind everyone again, that winter is past, and that spring brings new life. This custom was followed by the heathen people of the world, long before Jesus and Christianity came into being! We see these **decorated eggs, rabbits and hares** portrayed now on confectionery and greeting cards at every Easter time. It is just another deceitful plan of the enemy of God to integrate his pagan schemes into the Christian church!

HALLOWEEN

This too has its roots in the ancient Celtic festival of **Samhain**! (Pronounced **"SAH-win"**.) It was a pagan religious celebration to welcome the harvest at the end of summer in the Northern Hemisphere. People would light bonfires and wear all sorts of weird costumes and paint weird pictures, to ward off the ghosts and evil spirits. Now we see this happening in the Southern Hemisphere as well.

In the eighth century, Pope Gregory designated **the first of November**, as a time to honour the saints. Not long after this, **All Saints Day** came into being, incorporating some of the traditions of Samhain. The evening before All Saints Day came to be known as **All Hallows Eve**, and later evolved into **Halloween**.

As often happens, business enterprises see immense profits to be made in commercializing these festivals. Today we see incredible sales of XMAS trees with special lights and decorations, big and small blow-up images of Santa and all sorts of weird depictions of these festivals, to bring in huge profits for these businesses, capitalizing on the ignorance of the public as opportunity to make money!

Satan has blinded people to his nefarious efforts to integrate his schemes and practices into the lives of so many people, including wonderful Christian people who truly believe they are honouring our Creator and Redeemer, by incorporating these festivals into their lives.

For those who have a mind to investigate, there is abundant evidence for us to understand where these special times and celebrations have originated. God has provided and preserved evidence of the devil's arts. Therefore, we can thank our loving Heavenly Father for His warnings and alerts, so we can recognize the tactics of the enemy of God. His Word says,

"Be sober, be vigilant; because your adversary the devil, as a roaring lion, walketh about, seeking whom he may devour." 1 Peter 5:8

"Therefore, come out from among them and be ye separate, saith the Lord; touch not the unclean thing, and I will receive you." 2 Corinthians 6:17

God loves all His creation and all people, regardless of race, colour or creed, or however sinful we have been, His arms are open wide, waiting for anyone to come to Him to receive forgiveness and salvation.

"Come unto Me all ye that labour and are heavy laden. Take my yoke upon you and learn of me, for I am meek and lowly in heart, and ye shall find rest unto your souls." Matthew 11:29-30

"This is how God showed His love among us. He sent His Son into the world that we might live by Him. This is love; not that we loved God, but that He loved us and sent His Son as an atoning sacrifice for our sins. Dear friends, since God so loved us, we also ought to love one another." 1 John 4:9-11

"Give thanks unto the Lord, for he is good; His love endures forever." 1Chronicles 16:34

"Know therefore that the Lord your God is God; He is the faithful God, keeping His covenant of love to a thousand generations of those who love Him and keep His commandments." Deuteronomy 7:9 "

"I have loved you with an everlasting love; therefore, with loving kindness have I drawn you." Jeremiah 31:3

There are many, many more beautiful verses in God's Word, describing His unfathomable love for His people, and His Creation. May I encourage you all to read His Word, especially the Gospels, as He tries to draw all people to Himself.

With God behind you and His arms around you... you can face whatever is ahead of you...may God's loving arms carry you always near His heart.

Oh, what a LOVING Being is our God!

CHAPTER 41

THE LETTER

This chapter relates a very heart-moving story, which parallels our Heavenly Father's love for his beloved, the beings He created after His own image, after His own likeness; the beings He wanted to be with for the rest of eternity that has no end and no separation or divorce, ever. It really touched my heart when I first read it, and I'm sure you'll find it so as well.

Nothing other than our **choice,** or the plans of the enemy of God heeded to, can separate us from that amazing **LOVE.** Even if the enemy causes something to happen to prevent us from being with Him, His love remains steadfast. This story really demonstrates that kind of true love on God's part, and on the part of those who **choose** to <u>never doubt or stop loving Him.</u>

Dear **Job** during all the things Satan did to him; **Abraham** who was asked to sacrifice his only son; **Isaac** who trusted and obeyed his father implicitly; **Jacob** who had to work another seven years for his wife Rachel; **Daniel** even though he faced a den of lions; the **Three Hebrew Boys** facing the fiery furnace; and the list could go on and on, and it is still going on today! The love affair between God and His people is truly amazing!

Our God is a God of unquenchable **LOVE**, and I want to always remain faithful and true to Him as one of His people who truly love Him and will be ready to meet Him when He returns, and eventually to be among those who will make up **"His Bride"**, at the **Marriage Feast of the Lamb.** Check Paul's Letter to the **Ephesians in chapter 5: 22-33, and Revelation 19:7-9.**

Just as this dear couple had to wait for their marriage for nearly a lifetime, so **"Jesus, our Bridegroom"**, has been waiting for **"His Bride"** and **"His Marriage"** after a very long **courtship of almost six thousand years.** What a beautiful metaphor of true **LOVE!**

Author unknown!

"As I walked home one freezing day, I stumbled on a **wallet** someone had lost in the street. I picked it up and looked inside to find some identification so I could call the owner. But the wallet contained only **three dollars and a crumpled letter** that looked as if it had been in there for years. The envelope was worn and the only thing that was legible on it was the return address.

When I opened the letter, hoping to find some clue, I saw the dateline-**1924.** The letter had been written almost sixty years ago. It was written in a beautiful feminine handwriting on powder blue stationery with a little flower in the left-hand corner. It was a 'Dear John' letter that told the recipient, whose name appeared to be **Michael**, that the writer could not see him anymore because her mother forbade it. Even so, she wrote that she would always love him. It was signed, **Hannah.**

It was a beautiful letter, but there was no way except for the name Michael, that the owner could be identified. Maybe if I called information, the operator could find a phone listing for the address on the envelope.

"Operator," I began, "this is an unusual request. I'm trying to find the owner of a wallet that I found. Is there any way you can tell me if there is a phone number for an address that was on an envelope in the wallet?"

She suggested I speak with her supervisor, who hesitated for a moment then said, "Well, there is a phone listing at that address, but I can't give you the number." She said, as a courtesy, she would call that number, explain my story and would ask them if they wanted her to connect me. I waited a few minutes and then she was back on the line. "I have a person, who will speak with you."

I asked the woman on the other end of the line if she knew anyone by the name of Hannah. She gasped, **"Oh! We bought this house from a family who had a daughter named Hannah. But that was thirty years ago!"**

"Would you know where that family could be located now?" I asked.

"I remember that Hannah had to place her mother in a nursing home some years ago," the woman said. "Maybe if you got in touch with them, they might be able to track down the daughter."

She gave me the name of the nursing home and I called the number. They told me the old lady had passed away some years ago, but they did have a phone number for where they thought the daughter might be living.

I thanked them and phoned. The woman who answered explained that Hannah herself was now living in a nursing home.

This whole thing was stupid, I thought to myself. Why was I making such a big deal over finding the owner of a wallet that had only three dollars and a letter that was almost sixty years old?

Nevertheless, I called the nursing home in which Hannah was supposed to be living and the man who answered the phone told me, "Yes, Hannah is staying with us."

Even though it was already 10.00p.m, I asked if I could come by to see her. "Well," he said hesitatingly, "if you want to take a chance, she might be in the day room watching television." I thanked him and drove over to the nursing home.

The night nurse and a guard greeted me at the door. We went up to the third floor of the large building. In the day room, the nurse introduced me to Hannah.

She was a sweet, silver-haired old timer with a warm smile and a twinkle in her eye. I told her about finding the wallet and showed her the letter. The second she saw the powder blue envelope with that little flower on the left, she took a

deep breath and said,

"Young man, this letter was the last contact I ever had with Michael."

She looked away for a moment deep in thought and then said softly, "I loved him very much. But I was only sixteen at the time and my mother felt I was too young. Oh, he was so handsome. He looked like Sean Connery, the actor."

"Yes," she continued. "Michael Goldstein was a wonderful person. If you should find him, tell him I think of him often. And", she hesitated for a moment almost biting her lip, "tell him I still love him. You know," she added, smiling as tears began to well up in her eyes, "I never did marry. I never found anyone who matched up to Michael . . ."

I thanked Hannah and said goodbye. I took the elevator to the first floor and as I stood by the door, the guard there asked, "Was the old lady able to help you?" I told him she had given me a lead. "At least I have a last name. But I think I'll let it go for a while. I spent almost the whole day trying to find the owner of this wallet."

I had taken out the wallet, which was a simple brown leather case with red lacing on the side. When the guard saw it, he said, "Hey, wait a minute! That's

Mr. Goldstein's wallet. I'd know it anywhere with that bright red lacing. He's always losing that wallet. I must have found it in the halls at least three times."

"Who's Mr. Goldstein?" I asked as my hand began to shake.

"He's one of the old timers on the eighth floor. That's Mike Goldstein's wallet for sure. He must have lost it on one of his walks."

I thanked the guard and quickly ran back to the nurse's office. I told her what the guard had said. We went back to the elevator and got on. I prayed that Mr. Goldstein would be up. On the eighth floor, **the floor nurse said, "I think**

he's still in the day room. He likes to read at night. He's a darling old man."

We went to the only room that had any lights on and there was a man reading a book. The nurse went over to him and asked if he had lost his wallet. Mr. Goldstein looked up with surprise, put his hand in his back pocket and said, "Oh, it is missing!'

"This kind gentleman found a wallet and we wondered if it could be yours?"

I handed Mr. Goldstein the wallet and the second he saw it, he smiled with relief and said, "Yes, that's it! It must have dropped out of my pocket this afternoon. I want to give you a reward."

"No, thank you," I said. "But I have to tell you something. I read the letter in the hope of finding out who owned the wallet." The smile on his face suddenly disappeared. "You read that letter?"

"Not only did I read it, I think I know where Hannah is."

He suddenly grew pale. "Hannah? You know where she is? How is she? Is she still as pretty as she was? Please, please tell me!" he begged.

"She's fine . . . just as pretty as when you knew her," I said softly.

The old man smiled with anticipation and asked, "Could you tell me where she is? I want to call her tomorrow." He grabbed my hand and said, "You know something mister, I was so in love with that girl that when that letter came, my life literally ended. I never married. I guess I've always loved her."

"Mr. Goldstein," I said, "Come with me." We took the elevator down to the third floor. The hallways were darkened and only one or two little night-lights lit our way to the day room where Hannah was sitting alone watching the television. The nurse walked over to her.

"Hannah," she said softly, pointing to Michael, who was waiting with me in the doorway. "Do you know this man?" She adjusted her glasses, looked for a moment, but didn't say a word. Michael said softly, almost in a whisper, "Hannah, it's me, Michael. Do you remember me?"

She gasped, "Michael? I don't believe it! Michael? It is you! my Michael!"

He walked slowly towards her, and they embraced. The nurse and I left with tears streaming down our faces. About three weeks later I got a call at my office from the nursing home.

"Can you break away on Sunday to attend a wedding? Michael and Hannah

are going to tie the knot!"

It was a beautiful wedding with the people at the nursing home dressed up to join in the celebration. Hannah wore a light beige dress and looked beautiful. Michael wore a dark blue suit and stood tall. They made me their best man. The hospital gave them their own room and if you ever wanted to see a seventy-six-year-old bride and a seventy-nine-year-old groom acting like two teenagers, you had to see this couple."

It was a perfect ending for a love affair that had lasted nearly sixty years. I don't know about you, but this story of genuine **TRUE LOVE**, still brings tears to my eyes whenever I read it again.

Michael and Hannah's love had lasted **sixty years**. I see another amazing love affair that has lasted almost **six thousand years** of separation caused by the enemy of God.

Can you imagine the joy and celebration when the Fiancé and His betrothed are united again, with nothing to ever separate them again, forever?

Oh, what an amazing re-union that will be, when the **Bridegroom,** (Jesus), and His **Bride,** (those who truly love Him), are united again, and we can all rejoice at the **"Marriage Supper of the Lamb"!** Revelation 19:7-9 says,

"Let us be glad and rejoice and give honour to Him: for the marriage of the Lamb has come and His wife has made herself ready.

And to her was granted that she should be arrayed in fine linen, clean and white: for the white linen is the righteousness of saints.

And he, (the angel in John's vision), **said to me, "Write. Blessed are they which are called unto the Marriage Supper of the Lamb." And he said to me, "These are the true sayings of God."**

You and I can be part of the **"Bride of Christ".**

The courtship between God and man has been going on for nearly six thousand years. The Lord has been wooing mankind, who were made in His image, after His likeness. Like my wife and I, we have become old and don't look as lovely as when we first saw each other, and certainly not as beautiful as our first parents who God created and gave a beautiful home in Eden!

He **loves** all His creation so much, that He even sacrificed His only begotten Son, Jesus, to pay the price of sin, so that we could be re-united forever with Him, as He intended in the beginning. He has told us plainly that He offers redemption to **whosoever will** accept His infinite love.

In His love letter, the Scriptures, the Bible, He tells us that those who truly love and serve Him will have brand new, beautiful bodies, which will never again experience sickness, sorrow, or death.

Jesus' words, while He was here, and before He ascended to heaven after His resurrection, were the words of a most loving romantic suitor. Let's consider some of them once more, from the Old and the New Testaments, as we contemplate the enormity of God's **LOVE**.

John 14:1-3 "Let not your heart be troubled: you believe in God, believe also in Me.

In my Father's house are many mansions: if it were not so, I would have told you. I go to prepare a place for you.

And if I go and prepare a place for you, I will come again and receive you unto Myself; that where I am, there you may be also."

Psalms 36:7 "How priceless is your unfailing love, O God! People take refuge in the shadow of your wings."

Romans 5:8 "But God demonstrates His own love for us in this: while we were still sinners, Christ died for us."

1 John 4:10-12 "Herein is love, not that we loved God, but that He loved us, and sent His Son to be the propitiation for our sins.

Beloved, if God so loved us, we ought also to love one another.

No man has seen God at any time. If we love one another, God dwells in us, and His love is perfected in us."

Ephesians 3:19 "And to know the love of Christ, which passes knowledge, that you might be filled with all the fullness of God."

Jeremiah 29:11 "For I know the thoughts I think toward you, saith the Lord, thoughts of peace, and not of evil, to give you an expected end."

John 3:16 and 17 "For God so loved the world, that He gave His only begotten Son, that whosever believeth in Him should not perish, but have everlasting life.

For God sent not His Son into the world to condemn the world, but that the world through Him might be saved."

And there are so many more examples of the unfathomable **LOVE of God** in His **LOVE LETTER** to you and me, and all mankind, in His Holy Word, the Scriptures!

Another thing that really amazes me, is that He says He is going to re-create this tiny world, and make it His Headquarters of the Universe, and dwell with His people right here, on this earth, with His Bride, forever! What a Honeymoon that will be!

"Behold I stand at the door and knock: if any man hears My voice, and will open the door, I will come in to him, and will sup with him, and he with Me." Revelation 3:20

To join His family, begin by reading the Gospels; talk to Him daily, hourly; ask Him for forgiveness of any sins, and follow His commandments, not to earn His love, but to show Him how much you love Him.

Be an example to everyone as a child of the King. Share your love for God wherever you can. Use the talents God has given you, no matter how few or how small, to tell the Good News, (the GOSPEL) to anyone who'll listen!

Never be afraid to tell others of your love for our Heavenly Father, dear Jesus our Saviour and the Holy Spirit, who will empower you to be ambassadors for God. Tell everyone of His amazing and unfathomable LOVE.

Jesus' commission to His disciples was very implicit: See Mark 16:15-16 **"And He said unto them, Go ye into all the world, and preach the gospel to every creature."**

Won't you join with me in rejecting the enemy and choose to accept God's unfailing LOVE? Won't you join with me in sharing God's love with everyone? The wonderful offer of salvation is still available!

My Princess is holding a lovely illustration of the Bridegroom and His Bride, in garments clean and white, ready for the Marriage Supper of the LAMB!

Oh, what an amazing loving Heavenly Father Who is freely offering Salvation and Eternal Life in an Earth Made New, to Whosoever will accept His offer.

Using his servants the prophets, and His Holy Spirit, He has told us clearly how we can know that "**the end of this world**" is about to happen. As in the **TRUE AUSTRALIAN STORY**, we can know that we are almost at the "**Cliff Edge**".

So, let's "get our noses off the ground", be prepared ourselves, and share this vital loving message with whoever will listen.

There are **FOUR** very important questions we all have to answer sooner or later:

1. Where did we come from?

Are you **choosing** to believe that a loving Creator made our first parents, or did we evolve over millions of years from a Big Bang?

2. Why are we here?

Is it our purpose to glorify our loving Heavenly Father, or are we **choosing** to glorify and please ourselves?

3. How should we live?

Are we **choosing** to follow **all** of God's Ten Commandments, or just following the crowd and doing whatever we **choose**.

4. Where are we going?

Are we **choosing** eternal life with our Lord in an earth made new, or eternal annihilation with Satan and his followers?

"Where we go hereafter, depends on what we go after here!"

Won't you decide with me to follow the Great Shepherd Who gave His life to save His sheep. He has promised to lead us to green pastures beside still waters, where we will dwell with Him and enjoy life everlasting, in a brand-new re-created earth, where there will be no sign of sin, or suffering or death throughout eternity!

I love this picture of Jesus, the Good Shepherd, painted by a talented artist.

What a wonderful LOVING Saviour is our Lord!

THE GOOD SHEPHERD IS JESUS MY LORD, WHO REALLY LOVES HIS SHEEP.

The LORD is my shepherd; I shall not want.
He maketh me to lie down in green pastures:
He leadeth me beside the still waters.
He restoreth my soul:
He leadeth me in the paths of righteousness for His name's sake.
Yea, though I walk through the valley of the shadow of death,
I will fear no evil: for Thou art with me;
Thy rod and Thy staff they comfort me.
Thou preparest a table before me in the presence of mine enemies:
Thou anointest my head with oil; my cup runneth over.
Surely goodness and mercy shall follow me all the days of my life:
and I will dwell in the house of the LORD for ever.

PSALM 23 (The Bible)

I CAN UNHESITATINGLY SAY, IT'S ALL ABOUT LOVE!

THE LOVE LETTER FROM OUR HEAVENLY FATHER, HIS SON JESUS CHRIST AND THEIR HOLY SPIRIT.

ABOUT THE AUTHOR

Don Menkens was born in Townsville and grew up in North Queensland. After graduating from High School, he worked on his grandfather's cane farm for a year to earn enough money to go to Avondale College at Cooranbong, to train as a builder. From the age of ten he planned to work as a Missionary in the Islands of the Pacific to build schools and churches for the island people, where they could learn about God and His love.

Because he was only seventeen his work-study programme at Avondale soon devoured all his savings. He saw that he could not complete the Building Course, so for a while he tried Colporturing, but that was not successful either, because of the rainy season. So, on the advice of some friends, he enrolled at the Queensland Teachers College and completed the Teaching Course.

After working for the Queensland Education Department for a while, he was called by the Seventh Day Adventist Church to be Principal of the aboriginal school at Mona Mona, near Cairns, where he taught for two years, before being asked to take charge of a school at Belepa in the Papuan Gulf as Principal with seven staff.

He also pioneered a new school further round the Gulf on the Kikori River. Three hundred acres of tropical jungle and a budget of $300 was quite a challenge, but the school was established and is still operating today. He and his wife Ruth spent seven years in the hot wet steamy jungles of the Papuan Gulf before being transferred to Kabiufa High School and College near Goroka in the New Guinea Highlands for four years. What a very welcome change of climate that was!

With his wife Ruth and their five children they returned to Australia in 1973, so their older children could continue higher education in Australia. He was Principal of a new school he planned and organized at Mullumbimby for six years, before taking charge of Macquarie Fields school in Sydney for four years. He then was posted to Townsville and retired after a year there in 1984.

They bought a small acreage of land near Kingaroy and developed a small farm and Earthworm business for ten years. They also trained as Natural Health teachers and taught Swedish Massage at Kingaroy TAFE College for three years. They also helped set up Health Centres at Kangaroo Valley, in NSW, New Zealand on the Coromandel Peninsula, Living Valley near Kin Kin in Qld and elsewhere.

He lost his dear **Ruth** in 2016, after sixty-three years together, just before her eighty-first birthday. The Lord put her to sleep very peacefully but unexpectedly. How he found and married a lovely widow from the Blue Mountains, is told in this book and is quite a story! His new companion is **Naomi**. **Ruth** and **Naomi**? Hmmm! Now, they are enjoying retirement at Landsborough on the Sunshine Coast of Qld.

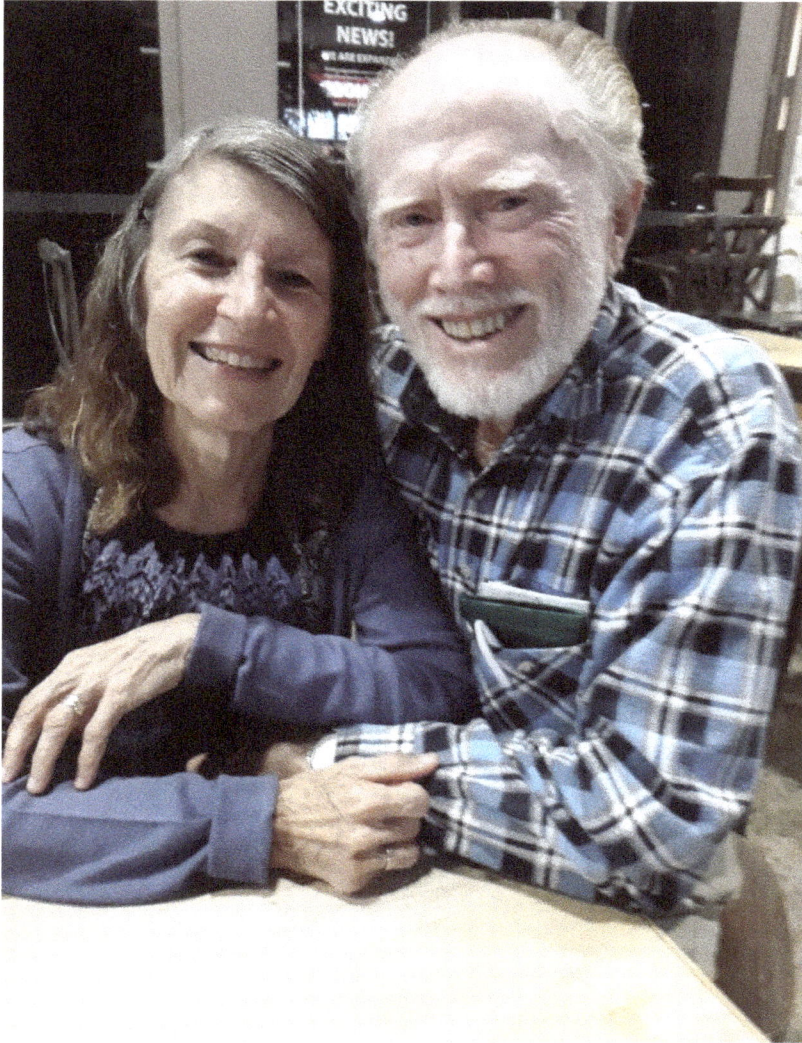

Don and Naomi